THE MASTER GARDENER'S GUIDE TO

VEGETABLE GROWING

All you need to know about growing
more than thirty vegetables to perfection

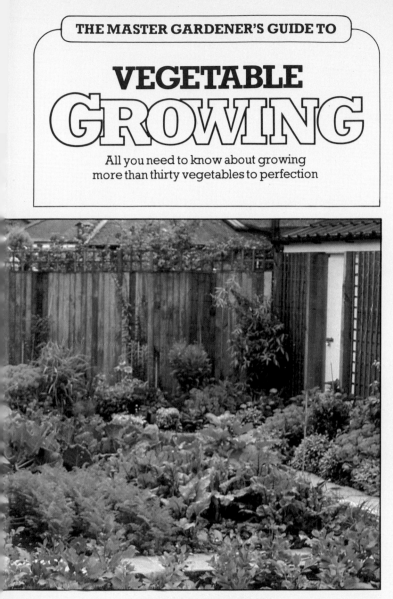

ELISABETH ARTER

SELECT
EDITIONS

A SALAMANDER BOOK

©1986 Salamander Books Ltd.

This edition published 1991 by
Selectabook Ltd.,
Folly Road,
Roundway,
Devizes,
Wiltshire, U.K.
SN10 2HR.

ISBN 0 86101 216 X

Credits
Editor: John Woodward
Designer: Kathy Gummer
Copy editor: Edward Bunting
Filmset: Modern Text Ltd.

Colour reproductions:
Melbourne Graphics
Printed in Belgium by
Proost International Book
Production, Turnhout

AUTHOR

Elisabeth Arter has been a horticultural writer for 20 years and an enthusiastic gardener since childhood. She is particularly interested in growing vegetables and spends a lot of time trying out new techniques and new varieties. She writes each month on vegetable growing in *Practical Gardening,* contributes regularly on various aspects of the hobby to a number of other national and provincial UK publications and is author of a book on salad vegetables. She has given many talks on gardening on local radio, and lectures on the subject to adult education evening classes.

Consultant

Ann Bonar has been a horticultural writer and consultant for more than 20 years, and has written many books on various aspects of gardening. She is a regular contributor to a variety of gardening periodicals and trade journals, and has taken part in a number of gardening programmes broadcast by the BBC. For 12 years she has answered readers' queries sent in to a leading British weekly gardening magazine.

CONTENTS

Home-grown vegetables help to cut housekeeping bills, give the family a more varied diet and provide fresh food at its most tasty and nutritious. You can harvest an impressive amount of produce from a very small area if you use modern space-saving high-yielding varieties, and if you put in one crop as soon as another is finished. Regular exercise in the open air as you tend the plot all year round is enjoyable and good for your health, though neither this nor the time you need to spend will be excessive if you follow the labour-saving tips in this book.

A vegetable plot can provide produce so fresh that no vitamins are lost between gathering and table; and can offer a wide choice of different crops and out-of-season luxuries that would be expensive to buy. When space is limited, you can concentrate all the more on growing those vegetables that deteriorate most quickly after harvesting, are seldom seen in the shops, or are needed frequently but in very small quantities.

Glass in various forms, or inexpensive polythene sheeting, helps to protect plants early and late in the year. This will result in a longer growing season, an earlier harvest when prices are highest, and the ability to grow those crops that cannot be guaranteed to do well in a poor summer. Starting seedlings under cover means earlier crops, particularly of the half-hardy vegetables, and gives more scope for following one crop with another as young plants raised in soil blocks or plant starters will mature well before those sown *in situ*.

QUICK RETURNS

Especially important are the quick return crops, ready to eat in a few weeks from starting, and ready to make way for something else after a short season. They can be grown as 'catch crops' before the main planting goes in.

Below: *Rows of beetroot, carrots and parsnips promise a fine crop of fresh, chemical-free vegetables.*

Spinach sown under cover in early spring or in the open in mid-spring will give many pickings before the plot is needed for midsummer planting of winter brassicas. Lettuce raised inside in plant starters and put out under cloches in early spring can be cut in late spring to make way for celery or maincrop runner beans. In a well-run vegetable garden the ground is never left idle, for follow-on sowings and plantings are made as soon as the previous crop is harvested and the land cleared.

Whether your garden is large or small, it is best to grow small quantities of a wide variety of different crops to avoid gluts, and to give continuity of supply and a choice for the table. Even so, aim at growing extra for peak periods such as the school holidays, and more of those crops you want to freeze for winter.

ENJOYABLE WORK

Some people are put off vegetable growing by the thought of the work involved, yet will spend many hours mowing, edging, feeding and generally caring for a lawn. A kitchen garden need involve no more work and, when properly organized, this can be a pleasant exercise all year.

Vacant land that has been manured, limed where necessary, and dug over in winter does not need a great deal of effort to be raked down into a tilth for spring sowing and planting. Work in the garden is enjoyable on light evenings and fine weekends, and, if jobs are tackled regularly, relatively little time need be taken up with hoeing, weeding and other routine chores.

Feed your soil and your growing crops well, be prepared to water them generously in dry weather, and you will produce healthy plants that give high yields. Early preventative measures against pests and diseases ensure that very little in the way of chemical controls will be necessary. One big advantage of growing at home is that you can have vegetables guaranteed free of chemical spray and dust residues that could be harmful.

GUIDE TO SEASONS

Throughout this book terms such as 'mid-spring' have been used instead of months, to allow for regional differences in climate. This chart shows appropriate months for northern and southern areas of the UK.

Season	South	North
Early spring	March	Late March/April
Mid-spring	April	May
Late spring	May	June
Early summer	June	July
Mid-summer	July	July
Late summer	August	August
Early autumn	September	September
Mid-autumn	October	October
Late autumn	November	October
Early winter	December	November/December
Mid-winter	January	January/February
Late winter	February	Early March

PLANNING AND SITING

Best results with vegetables can only be obtained on a prime site in the garden. Most people prefer this to be well away from house windows and screened from the sitting out area, but that's no reason to relegate these crops to the far end of the garden where conditions may not necessarily be ideal.

SELECTING A SITE

The best site is in a sunny, open position, with some shelter from strong winds. Avoid an area shaded by high buildings, near trees or a tall hedge. Drips from overhanging branches, shade cast by summer foliage and competition from active roots will reduce yields from vegetables. Other sites to avoid are frost pockets, where cold air collects to give lower temperatures, especially harmful in late spring when there is a lot of tender young growth.

Most vegetables do best on deeply dug, fertile soil, but a great deal can be done to improve any land, whatever the soil type, by regular cultivation and the working in of generous amounts of rotted organic matter. Much of this can be produced on a compost heap situated at one corner of the plot.

EASIER WORKING

For convenience and ease of cultivation, try to have all the vegetable growing area together. A few long rows are much easier to manage than many short ones. A good path with a con-crete or similar hard surface alongside is helpful, but any intersecting paths should be narrow and temporary, to economize on space and save work. As far as possible, rows should run north to south, to reduce the risk of runner beans or other tall crops shading the other vegetables.

Some irrigation will be needed every year, and it is worth investing in enough hosepipe to reach all the plot. It also helps to site a water butt nearby, which you can refill by hose for small applications by can.

HOW MUCH LAND?

The conventional British allotment measuring 30 x 90ft (10 x 30m) was reckoned sufficient land to feed a family of four all year. Few modern gardens allow that much room for culinary crops, but few gardeners today think it worth growing a year's supply of potatoes or large areas of winter cabbages for storage.

A very much smaller plot is still enough to keep a family in salads, luxury vegetables and quick return crops to stock the freezer for winter. Modern varieties of compact habit are economical of space, as are climbing beans, tall varieties of peas and outdoor cucumbers trained up netting.

It is often most convenient to have an area set aside for rhubarb and other perennial vegetables rather than grow them among the crops whose site will change annually.

A GOOD-LOOKING GARDEN

Growing crops can be screened temporarily with annual sweet peas or the scarlet runner beans that were introduced to Britain as a decorative crop; or permanently with cordon apples and pears, blackberries and other cane fruit, or climbing roses and clematis. It is often helpful to grow flowers for cutting among vege-tables, and rows of dahlias, early-flowering chrysanthemums or sweet peas for cut blooms can enhance the appearance of the culinary plot.

SELECTING TOOLS

Good quality tools make for easier working and are a worth-

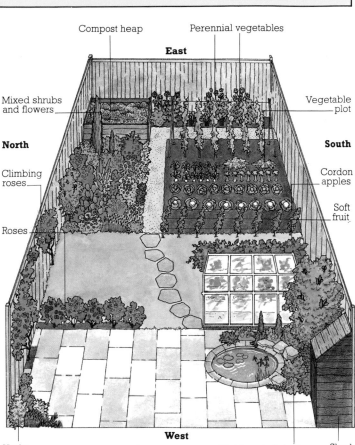

Compost heap   Perennial vegetables

East

Mixed shrubs
and flowers

Vegetable
plot

North   **South**

Climbing
roses

Cordon
apples

Soft
fruit

Roses

Herbs   Moisture and shade-   Shed
loving plants

West

while investment. It is far better
to start off with secondhand
but well-made tools than with
cheap new ones of inferior make.
Keep them clean, sharpened as
necessary, and always put them
back in the shed after use—
making sure that those with
cutting edges are stored away
from the reach of small fingers.

GARDEN REORGANIZATION

Whether you are starting a
new culinary plot, or hoping to
expand an existing area, it is
worth considering the value of
different features. How much
grass is necessary to give a lawn
for sitting out? Do some of your

Above: *A garden planned to give
ample room for growing vegetables and other culinary crops,
but allowing a good selection
of decorative plants and a sitting-
out area sited near the house.*

mature trees and large shrubs
occupy too much space? Would
a hedge be better replaced
with a fence that would give equal
privacy but which would entail
less maintenance, while not
competing for plant nutrients? Is
too much space given over to
paths? Replanning of this type
can often double the area for
vegetable growing without
reducing the decorative value
of the garden as a whole.

CROP ROTATION

It is wise to plan cropping so that different vegetables are grown on different parts of the plot in succession, for this makes best use of the plant foods in the soil and avoids a build up of pest and disease problems.

A THREE-YEAR PLAN

It is usual to plan for a three-year rotation with the plot split up into three sections. In the first year part 1 will be given over to the peas, beans, the onion family, spinach, celery and other crops that enjoy recently manured land; part 2 will be used for the cabbage family; and part 3 is for potatoes and roots.

Below: *In a classic rotation each plot is occupied in turn by legumes and onions, brassicas, and root crops, giving a full range of crops each year.*

Year 1

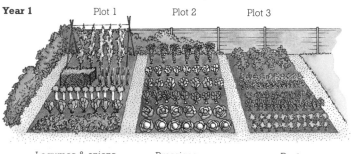

Plot 1   Plot 2   Plot 3

Legumes & onions   Brassicas   Roots

Year 2

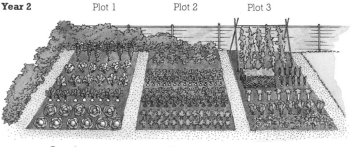

Plot 1   Plot 2   Plot 3

Brassicas   Roots   Legumes & onions

Year 3

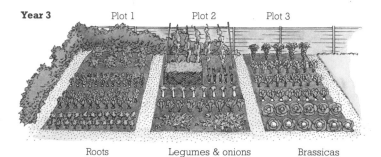

Plot 1   Plot 2   Plot 3

Roots   Legumes & onions   Brassicas

In the second year the cabbage family will move onto plot 1, the roots onto plot 2 and peas and other crops with similar needs onto plot 3. In the third year roots move onto plot 1, peas etc onto plot 2 and the cabbage family onto plot 3. In the fourth year the sequence starts over again.

Such a rotation should make weed control easier, as dense cover provided by brassica foliage, and earthing up around potatoes, has the effect of cleaning up the land as these crops rotate from plot to plot.

TIMING THE TREATMENTS

The area intended for the pea group is generously manured in the winter before they go in, and some gardeners like to double dig this section. The area intended for brassicas is given lime early in winter if the soil is at all acid, and later a light application of well-rotted organic matter plus fertilizers. The area intended for roots is given fertilizers only. Rotation thus ensures that the whole plot regularly receives manure, fertilizer and (where necessary) lime.

WORKING VARIATIONS

A three-year rotation works well in theory, but in practice it has to be adapted in order to fit everything into the plot, and allow for two or more crops growing on a particular site every year. For example, winter brassicas can follow early spinach, peas and beans in mid-summer, and main-crop beetroot and carrots can be sown in early summer after late broccoli and cauliflower are cleared. In this way the rotation is followed, but the cycle is completed in less than the three years.

The important thing is to try and group plants with like needs, and vulnerability to like pests and diseases, together, and make sure they do not grow on one part of the plot more often than necess-

ary. Exceptions are the perennial vegetables, which must, of course, stay in one place for some years; and runner beans that will grow in one spot for several years if the land is treated well.

PLANNING THE SEASON

Within the groups of different plants with like needs, there is a need to plan for a succession to maintain a supply through the season, and also to make sure that harvest dates coincide so that nearby rows can be cleared at one time to allow for a follow-on. Broad beans, first early peas, spinach and cloched lettuce will all be ready to clear by mid-summer and can be grouped together, while maincrop peas, dwarf beans and lettuce for late summer cutting are also good side by side.

The cabbage patch should be planned with autumn cabbage at one end and late spring cauliflower at the other, so that the crops are cleared in succession.

ROWS OR BLOCKS?

It is often most convenient to have long rows right across the plot, but that does not mean that each row has to be filled with just one type of plant. One broad drill can be divided into two lengths to take early carrots and beetroot, sown at the same time in early spring for harvesting and clearing by mid-summer, to make way for a late sowing of spinach and Chinese cabbage.

Alternatively, a long drill can be divided into short lengths of lettuce, spinach and spring onions sown in early spring to clear in time for sprouting broccoli to be planted in mid-summer.

Sweet corn and self-blanching celery are two crops better grown in blocks than long single lines, and there is a modern method where traditional rows are replaced with blocks of several short, closely-spaced rows; this is particularly good for carrots.

PREPARING THE GROUND

Digging and other major operations can seem very hard work if tackled in a hurry, and many a gardener has ended up with backache and blistered hands after working right through a spring weekend in an effort to prepare the whole plot for planting in one go.

WORKING TO A PLAN

Tackled steadily through the dormant season, on the other hand, land-preparing operations can be an enjoyable and healthy form of exercise. If the land is dug over early and left in rough clods, exposing the maximum soil surface to frost and winter weather, by springtime this texture is easy to break down into a tilth for seed beds. Land dug after the end of winter is better broken down as it is turned over.

The cold months are the best time, too, for such big jobs as cutting down trees, clearing shrubs, or grubbing out a hedge to make more room for culinary crops; for preparing a site for perennial vegetables, making or removing a path, or for putting up a fence. When the weather is unfit for outdoor work, tools can be sharpened and overhauled, the shed reorganized, potting composts mixed, a cropping plan prepared and seed orders for the coming season made up.

SINGLE DIGGING

Before starting to dig, clear away all weed growth and the remains of previous crops. Take up a trench 12in (30cm) wide and a spade's depth (one spit) across one end of the plot or, if a large area is to be dug, across one half of the end. For basic single digging, the technique is to turn over the next narrow strip of soil with a spade into this first trench; then, working in this way, go right across the plot until all the ground has been dug and there is a similar trench at the far end.

This is filled in with the soil dug out of the original trench; or in a large area divided into two, a new trench is taken out across the far end of the second half and soil from it is used for this filling. The second half of the plot is then dug over in the opposite direction until there is a trench at the first end that can be refilled with soil left there from the original trench.

DOUBLE DIGGING

This is not an essential, but much improves the depth of topsoil and is good on land that has not been cultivated for some years. The technique here is to take out a first trench of twice the width and to dig over the bottom with a fork before the next strip of topsoil is turned over into it. The same method is followed right across the plot until all the ground has been turned over to a depth of two spits. The job

Above: *A runner bean trench is dug to a full spade's depth—12in (30cm)—and twice this width. The technique is very similar to that used in double digging.*

is not too onerous if just a part of the plot is tackled each winter.

Whether single or double digging, it is important to keep the spade at right angles so that the maximum depth of land is dug, to turn the wrist as the spadeful of soil is lifted up so that this is turned completely over top to bottom, and to go slowly until a steady, easy rhythm is reached. Do not dig when the ground is frozen or very wet. Always clean off the spade with an old knife or piece of wood before putting it away.

LAYING DOWN MANURE

Manure or garden compost is best applied in autumn or winter, and wheeling this onto the plot is a good job for a frosty day when the land is too hard to dig. Spread it over the land before single digging so that the organic matter is worked in as this proceeds, but when double digging place manure into each trench as work proceeds so that it is dug into the lower spit.

PREPARING TRENCHES

Prepare a site for runner beans in winter by taking out a trench 12in (30cm) deep and twice this width. Spread a generous amount of rotted manure into the bottom and dig this in before replacing the topsoil.

The traditional varieties of celery that need blanching before use are also grown in a trench. Make this 12in (30cm) deep and 15in (37cm) wide, digging manure into the bottom and then replacing some topsoil to leave an open trench about 3in (8cm) deep.

If this job is done in winter, a row of cloched lettuce can be grown in the trench, and harvested before the celery is planted out, in early summer.

Above: *Spread a generous amount of well-rotted manure into the bottom of the trench, and then dig this into the ground below before replacing the topsoil.*

Above: *Sowing runner bean seeds in two drills in the prepared trench. Stout canes are put in to form supports for the plants before the seeds go in.*

MANURES AND FERTILIZERS

Manures and composts—the 'bulky organics'—provide plant nutrients and are good for improving the soil structure; but to get high yields of good vegetables, you need inorganic fertilizers as well.

MANAGEMENT OF MANURES

Farmyard and stable manure, poultry deep litter, spent mushroom compost and garden compost should be well rotted before being worked into the soil. Fresh manure mixed with straw is best added to the compost heap, or stacked to rot down for six months. Spent mushroom compost made largely from stable manure is already rotted and can be dug in right away.

These bulky organics are mainly spread on the ground in autumn and winter to be worked in during digging, but some very well-rotted compost can be worked in before spring or summer planting or used as a mulch for growing crops. They are very good for improving the soil structure, of both heavy and light land, and improve both drainage and moisture retention.

CHEMICAL FERTILIZERS

Nitrogen, phosphorus and potassium (commonly known as NPK) are the three main elements necessary for plant growth. These, in the form of fertilizers, are either raked into the soil as base dressings during final preparation of land for sowing or planting, or applied to the plants as top dressings, or as liquid or foliar feeds.

● **Nitrogen** promotes leafy growth and is applied mainly in spring and early summer. Later applications could delay flowering and fruiting or lead to soft growth that would not stand up to winter cold. Nitrogen leaches from the soil in heavy rain and so needs applying regularly, particularly after winter. It is contained in the quick-acting nitrate of soda, nitro-chalk and sulphate of ammonia. The organic hoof and horn fertilizer is a slow-release compound which supplies the element over some months.

● **Phosphorus** is needed for good root growth and for ripening fruit. Its most usual form is superphosphate of lime.

● **Potassium** helps a plant resist disease, water shortage and winter cold. Its most usual form is sulphate of potash. Some is available from wood ash collected from a bonfire or log-burning stove. Both this and phosphorus remain fairly constant in the soil.

NPK are also supplied as general, balanced compound fertilizers.

● In addition to the major elements, plants need traces of such elements as iron, magnesium, manganese, boron, copper, and molybdenum, but addition of trace elements is unlikely to be necessary for vegetables on soil regularly supplied with organic manures and not over-limed.

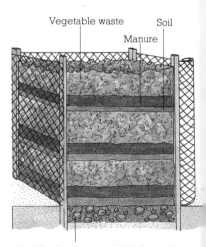

Vegetable waste   Soil

Manure

6in (15cm) twigs and rubble for drainage

Above: *A compost heap built on a 6in (15cm) layer of rubble topped by twigs for good drainage. The sides are of stout wire netting.*

LIME

The degree of acidity or alkalinity of soils is measured on the pH scale. This runs from 1 (acid) to 14 (alkaline), with 7 as neutral. Most vegetables grow best at a little below this, at 6.5. Acidity is corrected by the application of lime in the form of ground limestone spread on the soil surface in autumn or winter to be washed in by rain. It should not be applied at the same time as manure or fertilizers. Lime defiency causes club root in brassica crops. The need for lime can be checked by using a proprietary soil testing kit, which will also include advice on the quantity needed by a particular piece of land.

THE COMPOST HEAP

All kinds of household and garden waste, except diseased or woody material, can be made into garden compost together with litter from rabbit hutches or hen houses. Do not put into compost any plant material that has been treated with persistent hormone weedkillers; also be sure to exclude vegetables that are riddled with pest larvae.

Proprietary compost bins are neat and tidy, but in fact are usually too small to make large amounts of plant food or to heat up sufficiently to kill disease spores or weed seeds. A compost bin is easily constructed from four corner stakes and wire netting, or wooden slats. It should measure at least 36in (1m) square and a similar height, be covered for protection from heavy rain and have side ventilation. The ideal is to have two bins so that one can be started when the other is in the final stage of rotting down and being dug out.

Fill the bin with vegetable waste, plus animal manure when available, in layers 6-9in (15-22cm) deep with thin layers of about one inch (2·5cm) of soil in between. When no animal manure is available, a sprinkling of sulphate of ammonia or a proprietary compost activator can be used to assist the process.

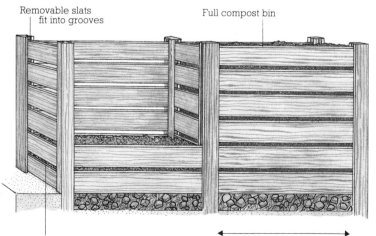

Removable slats fit into grooves

Full compost bin

Ventilation between slats

1yd (1 metre)

Above: *A structure of wooden slats fitted into grooved corner posts to allow easy removal makes a more efficient container.*

The heap should be covered against rain. Using two containers allows one heap to be built up while the other is rotting down.

Before seeds are sown in the open garden the soil must be broken down into a crumbly tilth, free of lumps and stones. Land dug before the winter frosts can be worked down into a tilth quite easily by going over the top few inches with a rake; base dressings of fertilizer can be incorporated into this upper layer during the final raking. Land dug nearer sowing time can be broken down with a hand or mechanical cultivator and then raked.

FINAL PREPARATIONS

On very light soil it may be necessary to consolidate the site by treading as a final preparation of the seedbed, but on wet or heavy soils it is important to tread on the ground as little as possible to avoid compacting the soil. If a seedbed is prepared, but there is no time to sow seeds the same day, cover the land with polythene sheet weighed down with stones or boards to protect from overnight rain.

WHEN TO SOW

Do not follow published gardening calendars slavishly. Sowings can be made 'early' in the sheltered south, but may have to be several weeks 'late' in cold northern districts. In late springs delay sowing until the soil has dried out and warmed up, rather than sow in cold wet earth where many seeds would rot.

SOWING THE SEED

Once the seedbed has been prepared, stretch a garden line tightly across the site and use the edge of a draw hoe against this to make shallow narrow drills for small seeds. Use the width of the blade instead if you want to make a broad shallow drill.

In dry weather, water the open drill before sowing to assist germination. Sow the seeds at

Left and above: *Sticks mark the ends of each seed drill (top left). The edge of the hoe is used to prepare a narrow drill for small seeds (left), which are then sown thinly in the bottom (below left). The seed drill is then covered with soil using a rake (above).*

the required depth and spacing, as set out in the individual entries later in this book. Fill in the drill with the rake after sowing, taking care not to cover the seed too deeply. Mark each end of every row and add a label with the name and variety of crop. Large seeds can be sown in individual holes made with a narrow trowel rather than in drills.

In the days after sowing, if the weather is dry, you may need to water each evening to assist germination.

THINNING THE SEEDLINGS

As soon as the seedlings are clearly visible, pull out any weeds and thin the crop so each tiny plant has room to develop, and to reduce the risk of damping-off fungal disease. Do this when the soil is damp from rain or watering and water again after the job has been completed.

PROTECTED SOWING

To give an early yield of vegetables, and a long enough season for half-hardy crops, seeds can be sown in a frame, in a greenhouse, or on a window-sill indoors. Small seeds such as celery can be sown in pans of one part peat and one part sharp sand or perlite, covering very thinly and keeping the medium moist until seedlings emerge.

As soon as they are large enough to handle, prick them out into seed trays, individual pots, soil blocks, or planting strips to grow on until large enough, or the weather is warm enough, for them to be planted in the open garden.

Large seeds such as marrows can be sown individually in pots or soil blocks, which permit them to grow on without root disturbance when they are transplanted later on.

An alternative method with small seeds is to sow a tiny pinch of seed in each soil block, or parts of a plant starter block of pots, for later thinning to one seedling per station.

PURCHASING SEED

Winter is the time for ordering seed supplies for the year ahead, for then you have first choice of varieties. F1 Hybrids are costly, but the vigour, uniformity and quality of the plants they produce justifies the price. Look for compact dwarf varieties if your garden is small, and for those bred for resistance to disease.

Most vegetable seeds (parsnip is an exception) will remain viable for two or three years, especially if packed in foil packets and stored in a dry cool place between seasons. This cuts cost and is especially helpful when you need only a few plants of one variety per year. For example, with brassicas it is better to grow ten plants of ten varieties than long rows of a few kinds.

Some seeds have been pre-treated with fungicide. They should be used up in one season, and after handling them you should always wash your hands.

PLANTING

When transferring plants from one medium to another they must be handled with great care, so that they recover from the move quickly with little check to their growth. **Prepare the site well, disturb roots as little as possible, and ensure that there is sufficient moisture for new roots to form rapidly.**

EARLY CROP

For earliest summer vegetables in the open or under cloches, the seeds are first germinated in gentle heat in the greenhouse or on a windowsill indoors; the seedlings are then moved outside, after hardening off, as sturdy young plants. For the most satisfactory results make use of individual pots, soil blocks, or planting strips that hold five seedlings comfortably.

Water the compost in these containers a few hours before planting, and each seedling can then be lifted out with a ball of compost that does not disintegrate, so that roots are hardly disturbed at all.

The site intended for young plants need not be worked down into a fine tilth as you would for seed sowing, but should be raked free of stones and lumps of earth and be reasonably level. Make a planting hole large enough to take the root ball, drop this in carefully, firm and water should the weather be dry.

Do not attempt to plant in cold wet soil, nor put in seedlings that have been under cover when there are very cold winds or low temperatures.

HALF-HARDIES

Some half-hardy vegetables can be sown direct into the open garden, but with protected sowing they will have a longer growing season and produce a better crop. The seedlings cannot be moved outside until frost risk is past, usually at the end of spring, but can be several weeks earlier if plants can go under cloches or be given some other temporary cover.

Large seedlings that go in some distance apart, such as courgettes, can be given individual night covers made from halved two-litre transparent plastic soft drink containers.

Below: *Planting cabbages with a narrow trowel. Each has been lifted with a good ball of moist soil around the roots (top). Those planted in autumn for spring cutting go in much closer (bottom).*

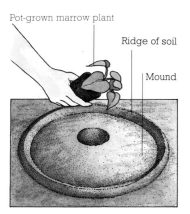

Pot-grown marrow plant
Ridge of soil
Mound

Water away from stems

Above: *Planting a pot-grown marrow into a prepared station. Water the compost in the pot a few hours before planting so the roots are* *not disturbed. Water with the rose off the can in the days after planting to avoid wetting the centre of the young plant.*

The weather will be warmer and drier when the half-hardies are planted, so they will probably need watering two or three times a week until established.

TRANSPLANTING FROM THE SEEDBED

Leeks and most of the cabbage family are normally raised in short rows in a seedbed for transplanting to the main site as well-developed seedlings. To assist a successful move from the seedbed grow them well, thinning if necessary to 1-2in (2.5-5cm) apart, and water the drill well the night before planting.

Lift with a fork to avoid breaking roots. Plant as soon as possible afterwards, using a trowel to make a hole large enough to allow the roots of the seedling to be spread out well. Replace the soil and firm in with the heel of your shoe. Tug a leaf of a young cabbage to check that it has been firmly planted.

Ideally, planting should be tackled in cool showery weather, but if it has to be done in a hot spell you can plant in the evening; for the next few days, shade plants from mid-day sun with sheets of newspaper.

Water after planting and give a ¼pt (150ml) of water a day to each cabbage plant for the next three to four weeks if the weather is dry. Research has shown that they move best at around six weeks and that the yield, particularly for cauliflowers, may be reduced if they are left in the seed row for much longer.

For leeks, make individual holes with a dibber, drop pencil-thick seedlings in, water with the can minus its rose and do not replace soil or firm.

PLANTING PERENNIALS

Perennial vegetables are going to stay in one place for years, and so the land for them must be prepared particularly well. Double dig the site, working a generous amount of rotted organic matter into the lower spit and making sure that all traces of perennial weeds have been removed. Rhubarb and globe artichokes are best planted in late winter and asparagus in spring, but you should prepare their sites some weeks in advance so the roots can go in without delay when they arrive from the nursery.

WATERING

Growing vegetables must be watered if you are to reap a good harvest, and especially so if you have free-draining soil, or the season is dry. Not all crops need the same treatment, and it may be a waste of time and water to give everything the same amount at the same time.

WATER-LOVING VEGETABLES

As a general rule the plants we grow for their leaves and stems—the members of the cabbage family, lettuce, celery, and spinach—need frequent watering throughout growth if the weather is at all dry. You will probably need a large can or two, full of water, for every square yard (metre) of land in summer. With cabbages, generous watering in the fortnight before the expected harvest date will greatly increase yield.

SPECIAL NEEDS

Root crops may make too much leaf if given too much water too often, while erratic watering from rain, or the can, will lead to split roots. Here the aim should be to give smaller amounts every two or three weeks all season to ensure steady growth with no checks.

Early potatoes are best watered every fortnight throughout growth, but need irrigation most from the time tubers are marble size until harvest.

Onions grown for bulbs need ample water in the early stages, but will not ripen well if given too much from mid-summer on.

Crops grown for their fruits—the peas and beans, tomatoes and sweet corn—need water most during the period from first flowering until picking.

It is vitally important to make sure all crops are watered well in the first weeks after transplanting, and to keep seedbeds moist for the late spring and summer sowings.

Above: *Lettuces need plenty of moisture throughout the growing period, but it is important to avoid wetting centres of maturing plants, as this may introduce rot.*

CONSERVING MOISTURE

The need for watering is reduced, and crops develop better, if the moisture-retaining property of light and porous land is improved by digging in plenty of organic matter. Moisture can be conserved in summer by mulching growing crops with peat, black polythene, or lawn mowings that have not been treated with weedkillers.

WATERING IMPLEMENTS

Individual plants and small plots can be watered with a can, but a hand-held hose, or sprinkler on a long spike, saves a great deal of effort. If you do rely on a can it may be possible to site a water butt, that can be refilled by hose, near the vegetable plot.

Crop	When to water	How often	Quantity*
Beans (all)	1st flowers to harvest	Weekly	4 (18)
Beetroot	Throughout growth	Every 2-3 weeks	2 (9)
Brussels sprouts	In month after planting In dry early autumn	Daily Weekly	¼ pt (150ml) per plant 4 (18)
Cabbage	In dry spells	Weekly	Up to 4 (18)
Calabrese	In dry spells	Weekly	Up to 4 (18)
Carrot	Throughout growth	Every 2-3 weeks	2 (9)
Cauliflower	In dry spells	Weekly	Up to 4 (18)
Cauliflower (late)	In month after planting In dry early autumn	Daily Weekly	¼ pt (150ml) per plant 4 (18)
Celery (all)	All season	Weekly	Up to 4 (18)
Courgette	Throughout growth	Twice weekly	2 (9)
Cucumber (outdoor)	Throughout growth	Twice weekly	2 (9)
Leaf beets	In all dry spells	Weekly	Up to 4 (18)
Leek	After planting	Weekly	Up to 2 (9)
Lettuce	Throughout growth	Weekly or more	Up to 4 (18)
Marrow	Throughout growth	Twice weekly	2 (9)
Onion (bulb)	Early life/dry spells	As needed	2 (9)
Onion (salad)	Throughout growth	Weekly	2 (9)
Parsnip	Throughout growth	Every 2-3 weeks	2 (9)
Potato (early)	All season when dry	Fortnightly	4 (18)
Spinach	Throughout growth	Weekly or more	Up to 4 (18)
Sprouting broccoli	In month after planting	Daily	¼ pt (150ml) per plant
Sweet corn	From flowering	Weekly	4 (18)
Tomato (outdoor)	After planting From flowering	Weekly or more Weekly or more	2 (9) 2 (9) or more
Turnip (early)	Throughout growth In dry spells	Weekly Weekly	2 (9) 2 (9)

*gals/sq yd (litres/m) or per plant

23

PROTECTED CROPPING

Every gardener needs some form of protection to extend the season at either end, help bring vegetables through the winter, and give better results with half-hardy summer crops.

CLOCHES

Traditional cloches with wire supports and two sheets of glass in the tent style or four sheets in the larger barn style give best protection from frost. They are costly to buy and to repair when the glass breaks, as it so easily does, and this can be a hazard, especially to young children.

At the other extreme are polythene tunnels with wire hoop supports and a continuous length of thin plastic sheet cover. They are inexpensive, and although they will not keep out much frost, they do warm up the ground very well and protect the plants from cold winds and birds. Plastic needs replacing after a couple of seasons, but one big roll will recover the hoops many times.

In between these two types are a variety of cloches made from rigid plastic, and the home handyman can often contrive his own to cut costs.

COLD FRAMES

Frames may be made from glass or polythene. Some have solid sides of wood or brick; others have both top and sides in aluminium and glass or polythene. They can be quite expensive and cannot be moved around the plot as easily as cloches, but they have many uses. Again the handyman can often make his own frame.

CROPPING PLAN

Plan planting so that cloches and frames are occupied through most of the year. Use the chart to work out a rotation: for example, cloches can cover lettuce in the spring, then tomatoes for a few weeks before sweet peppers from summer until mid-autumn; finally, they can cover the over-wintered spinach.

Below: *Sweet peppers are a good crop for growing under cloches in June to September from plants raised earlier in gentle heat.*

Crop	Stage to cover	Months to cover	Spacing plants x rows
Aubergines/ peppers	Planting to harvest	5-10	16 x 18in (40 x 45cm)
Beans: broad	Early life	11 or 2-4	4½ x 18in (11 x 45cm)
Beans: french	Early life	4-6	3 x 18in (8 x 45cm)
Beans: runner	Early life	4-6	6 x 24in (15 x 60cm)
Beetroot	Early crop	2-5	2 x 8in (5 x 20cm)
Brussels sprouts	Seedlings	2-4	½ x 6in (2 x 15cm)
Summer cabbage	Seedlings	2-4	½ x 6in (2 x 15cm)
Summer cauliflower	Seedlings	2-4	½ x 6in (2 x 15cm)
Carrots	Early crop	2-6	½ x 6in (2 x 15cm)
Celery: trench	Seedlings	4-6	1½ x 1½in (4 x 4cm)
Celery: self-B	Throughout	4-11	10 x 10in (25 x 25cm)
Chicory: S-L/R-V	Over winter	11-3	10 x 12in (25 x 30cm)
Corn salad	Over winter	9-4	5 x 5in (12 x 12cm)
Courgettes/marrows	Early life	4-0	30 x 30in (1m x 1m)
Cucumbers: outdoor	Early life	4-6	18 x 18in (45 x 45cm)
Land cress	Over winter	9-4	4 x 4in (10 x 10cm)
Leeks	Seedlings	2-6	½ x 6in (2 x 15cm)
Lettuce	Early and late season	9-6	10 x 10in (25 x 25cm)
Mustard and cress	Throughout	3-4 and 10-11	Sow thinly in patch
Peas	Early life late season	11-4 and 2-5	2x2x18in (5x5x45cm)
Potatoes	Early life	2-6	12 x 12in (30 x 30cm)
Radishes	Early crop	2-4	½ x 6in (2 x 15cm)
Salad onions	Early crop	2-6	½ x 6in (2 x 15cm)
Spinach	Over winter	11-4	6 x 12in (15 x 30cm)
Sweet corn	Early life	4-6	12-18in sq (30-45cm sq)
Tomatoes	Planting to flowering	5-6	15 x 15in (37 x 37cm)

PESTS AND DISEASES

Good strong plants with the right nutrients and spacing will stand up well to attack from pests or diseases; nevertheless watch out for early signs of trouble and make use of cultural controls wherever possible.

Using chemical controls as a routine measure is an unnecessary effort and expense, and they can destroy helpful insects that aid pollination or kill off pests, and leave residues that may be harmful.

Disease	Symptoms
Club root	Swollen roots of brassicas. Wilting in hot weather. Discoloured leaves
Damping off	Seedlings of many vegetables fail to emerge, or soon die
Downy mildew	Yellow patches on leaves, white or brown areas on undersides. Affects young brassicas, late lettuce, onions, peas
Powdery mildew	Powdery spots on leaves

Pests	Symptoms
Ants	Wilting plants. Ant hills near crops
Birds	Seedlings pulled out, or very damaged. Mature winter crops of brassicas eaten. Pea pods ripped open
Chafer grubs	Roots chewed below soil level mid-summer to mid-autumn. Problem on plot newly made from grassland
Cutworms	Stems eaten at soil level early spring to early autumn. Holes in root crops and potatoes
Leatherjackets	Stems attacked at soil level. Lower leaves eaten. Root crops tunnelled. Worst on light soil in wet weather
Millipedes	Seed, stems of young plants, roots and tubers eaten. Millipedes nearby
Slugs and Snails	Seedlings eaten, leaves, stems and roots of older plants damaged. Worst in damp weather. Slime trails present
Wireworms	Stems chewed through below soil level. Narrow tunnels in root crops and potatoes. Worst on land that was recently grass
Woodlice	Seedlings and young plants in frames attacked and killed or chewed

When pesticides or fungicides are needed, use the safest and least persistent, follow the manufacturer's instructions with care, wash out containers well and store materials in a safe place, clearly labelled, and well away from children.

Pests and diseases that affect a broad range of crops appear in this chart. Those attacking specific crops are listed in the entry for the vegetable concerned, later in this book.

Cultural control	Chemical control
Keep plot adequately limed and drained. Do not grow brassicas on site for several years after severe attack	Dip roots of transplants in benomyl solution before planting
Do not sow in cold wet soil. Use sterilized composts for indoor sowings. Sow thinly. Water and ventilate with care	Water with Cheshunt compound
Avoid overcrowding, rotate crops, use resistant lettuce varieties	Spray with Dithane at first sign of trouble
Remove affected leaves	Spray with benomyl

Cultural control	Chemical control
Scatter hills to reveal pests to birds. Apply boiling water	Dust affected affected area of with pyrethrum-based ant killer
Black thread between sticks over seed bed. Humming line to keep off small birds. Netting over winter greens and mature peas.	
Keep land clean and weed-free. Fork or rake over former grass often to reveal grubs to birds	Rake in Bromophos before sowing or planting 2in 5cm deep
Search soil near damaged plant, preferably at night. Destroy caterpillars	Rake in Bromophos as above.
Clear land and dig before end of September, especially if it was grass	Rake in Brompohos as above
Search soil near damaged plants and destroy the millipedes	Work Gamma-HCH into soil, but not for potatoes and roots
Trap with beer in shallow dishes. Encourage frogs and hedgehogs to garden	Put down small heaps of methiocarb pellets, protected from birds and pets. Pellets give some control against leatherjackets, millipedes and woodlice
Do not grow roots or potatoes for first two years after making plot from grassland. Turn over soil frequently to reveal pests to birds	Rake in Bromophos as above for some control
Collect and destroy pests	Use slug or ant killer

GLOBE ARTICHOKES

Globe artichokes are cousins of the thistle with ornamental greyish leaves and immature flower buds, parts of which form a luxury vegetable. They take up a lot of space for a small yield, but are not difficult to grow. The plants can be grown in a perennial border for the decorative value of silvery arching leaves among bright summer flowers.

HISTORY

Believed to have originated in Asia, globe artichokes have been cultivated in southern Europe for centuries. Grown in northern Europe since the 16th century, they tended to be a food of the wealthy in the past and were much grown in private gardens.

FOOD VALUE

The heads contain iron, mineral salts and some vitamins.

SOWING AND PLANTING

Choose a sunny, sheltered site on fertile, well-drained soil. Dig the land well in winter and work in plenty of well-rotted organic material, then rake in a dressing of general fertilizer a couple of weeks before you plan to plant.

Put in rooted offsets in early or mid-spring. These may be bought in, or cut away from the outsides of healthy high-yielding established clumps with a sharp knife. Each should be about 9in (22cm) long with some roots attached. Plant the offsets firmly 2in (5cm) deep at 2½ft (75cm) apart, water them well until they are established, then feed with a nitrogenous fertilizer six weeks later.

AFTERCARE

Apply a mulch in late spring to conserve moisture and keep down weeds. Throughout the summer keep the bed weed-free, and water in dry weather. Single heads will appear late in the season, and a mature plant will yield up to six heads.

Harvest the artichokes when the terminal bud is large and swollen, but still green and unopened. Feed and if necessary water the plants after the first cutting and more smaller secondary buds will appear later in the season.

In autumn cut down the dead stems, and earth up and cover the plants with straw or bracken to protect from frost. Make a new bed every third year, or replace one third of the bed each year. Plants left to crop for four or more years produce smaller, tougher artichokes.

Below: *Harvest globe artichokes by removing the terminal buds when they are plump and swollen, but still green and unopened.*

JERUSALEM ARTICHOKES

Above: *Jerusalem artichokes make tall sunflower-like plants in summer and must be supported with canes, or stakes, and twine.*

Above: *Jerusalem artichokes do not store well, so it is best to dig them as needed from mid-autumn through to spring.*

Jerusalem artichokes are perennial relations of the sunflower with knobbly, tuberous roots that make good winter soup. The plants are easy to grow and make a good summer screen and windbreak, but when left in from year to year growth becomes overcrowded and tuber quality deteriorates.

HISTORY

Originating in North America, and grown in Britain and France since the 17th century, the Jerusalem artichoke is thought to be so named because of a supposed resemblance in taste between the roots and globe artichokes, but botanically there is no connection. Nor is there any connection with Jerusalem, this part of the name probably having been derived from the Italian word *girasole* for sunflower.

FOOD VALUE

The tubers contain sodium, potassium, calcium, thiamin, and Vitamin C.

SOWING AND PLANTING

Not fussy about site or soil, Jerusalem artichokes do best on fertile land. Grow on the north side of the plot to avoid them shading other crops. Plant tubers the size of a hen's egg in late winter to spring, at 5in (13cm) deep and 1ft (30cm) apart. Before planting, dig over the site thoroughly and incorporate some well-rotted organic matter.

AFTERCARE

The plants will grow to 6ft (2m) or more high, and the stems should be supported with canes and twine in summer. This is easier if they are grown against a fence. A mulch of organic matter and watering in dry spells, plus liquid feeding on poorer land, boosts tuber quality. Cut the stems down in mid-autumn and lift tubers as needed through winter, saving some for replanting. The tubers can be stored, but quality deteriorates quickly and so it is best to cook them soon after lifting. It is very important to lift even the tiniest artichokes and plant back only a selection of good shape and size, as this maintains quality in future seasons.

ASPARAGUS

Asparagus needs to grow for several years before the first good harvest, so it is a poor choice for a small plot, or for anyone who makes frequent changes of home. But once started, a well-maintained bed will go on cropping for up to twenty years.

HISTORY

A member of the lily family that grows wild around the coasts of Europe, asparagus was eaten by both the ancient Greeks and Romans.

FOOD VALUE

Nutrients contained in the spears include calcium, iron, phosphorus, potassium and sulphur.

SITE AND SOIL

Choose an open position on well-drained soil that is not deficient in lime and is free of all perennial weeds. Dig a 2-3in (5-8cm) layer of well rotted organic material into the top spit of soil in the autumn before planting. The crop used to be grown in raised beds, but modern research has shown that asparagus grows best in three-row flat beds with plants spaced at 1ft (30cm) apart each way.

SOWING AND PLANTING

Older varieties are sown as seed in the open in early to mid-spring; the seedlings are thinned to 6in (15cm) apart to give crowns for moving to a permanent site the following spring. But the older varieties are not nearly as good as the best modern hybrids from France, which are available only as crowns and therefore involve less time.

Most asparagus beds are made up of male and female plants, the berrying females not yielding such a good harvest of spears as the males, and if fruits are allowed to ripen there are often self-sown seedlings to weed out. The new variety 'Lucullus' is male only and has overcome the problem.

It is best to buy one-year-old crowns, for these will recover from the move more satisfactorily than the older crowns sometimes offered. Plant in early or mid-spring, taking out a trench 8in (20cm) deep and 1ft (30cm)

Asparagus crowns   Heavy mulch   Asparagus shoots

12in (30cm)

Above: *Fleshy roots of the crowns should be spread out carefully at planting time. Top dress the bed every autumn with a thick layer of well-rotted manure, or garden compost. Cut plump asparagus spears from an established bed with a sharp knife about 1in (2.5cm) below soil level from mid-spring to early summer.*

Above: *Allow asparagus fern to grow up after cutting ceases early in summer, supporting the stems with canes and twine.*

wide for each row, replacing half the soil to give a ridge along the middle and placing the crowns on this with roots spread out well. Cover with 2-3in (5-8cm) of soil.

Protect the crowns by covering with a piece of damp cloth while you work, so that the fleshy roots do not dry out. Top dress the finished bed with 3oz (75g) per sq yd (m) of general fertilizer.

AFTERCARE

Hand weed the bed, as the roots grow near the soil surface and are easily damaged by hoeing. Water in dry spells. Support the asparagus fern with canes and twine. When the fern turns yellow in autumn, cut it down to near the ground and top dress the bed with a 2-3in (5-8cm) layer of well rotted manure or garden compost, which will complete the filling of the planting trench.

Repeat this organic feeding

every autumn and give a similar top dressing of fertilizer early every spring and again at the end of each cutting season. The ferns will need supporting each year from early summer to mid-autumn.

HARVEST

Do not cut any asparagus in the year after planting, and only a very little if growth looks really good in the second spring. In the third year from planting, harvest spears when they are 5-6in (13-15cm) long, using a sharp knife and cutting 1in (2½cm) below the soil surface, between mid-spring and early summer. In the years after that, cut over an eight-week season extending to mid-summer.

PESTS AND DISEASES

Slugs may be troublesome in spring (see general section on *Pests and Diseases,* page 26). Handpick the orange and black asparagus beetle and its grey-green larvae that strip foliage and stems, or control by dusting or spraying with derris. Weak, spindly spears are due to cutting too soon or lack of feeding.

Above: *A plump asparagus spear, ready to cut for eating. Some of the new season's fern has already been allowed to grow up from the weaker shoots.*

BROAD BEANS

Broad beans can be one of the earliest summer vegetables, are little trouble to grow, and good for freezing as well as eating fresh. Always gather pods while the beans are young, with no tendency to hard skins.

FOOD VALUE

The beans are a good source of protein, so an excellent crop for the vegetarian to grow; they also provide carbohydrate, Vitamin C, iron and dietary fibre.

SOWING AND PLANTING

A sunny open site on well-drained soil that has been dug and manured in autumn is best for the crop. The early harvest is by far the most important and for this you can sow in mid to late autumn to overwinter in the open in milder areas, or with cloche cover in colder parts, until mid-spring.

A late winter-early spring sowing is more reliable, but will be not ready until 2-3 weeks later unless given cloche cover.

Planting seeds in deep trays or plant starters in a greenhouse or cold frame in late winter, to transplant outside in early to mid-spring, speeds progress and is advisable if late winter is snowy or very wet. Sow 2in (5cm) deep in a drill or in individual holes made with a narrow trowel, at 4½in (11cm) apart with 18in (45cm) between the rows.

AFTERCARE

Top dress autumn-sown plants with 1oz (25g) per sq yd (m) of quick-acting nitrogen fertilizer at the end of winter, and hoe a similar dressing in around spring-sown beans once growth has started. Most varieties will need cane and twine supports from flowering until harvest.

PESTS AND DISEASES

If mice are a problem in the garden put down traps (inaccessible to birds) near seed drills. Blackfly can be largely avoided by growing only the early crop, and picking out the tops of the plants after flowering, or at the first sign of trouble.

Above: *Taller varieties of broad bean will need supporting with canes, or small stakes, and two or three lengths of twine.*

Above: *Dwarf varieties of broad bean are particularly suitable for growing under cloches, but should be uncovered before flowering.*

FRENCH BEANS

Most French beans are dwarf bushy plants, but some varieties climb like runner beans. The chief value of the crop is to give an early harvest before the better-flavoured runners. New varieties have round curved pods which are less stringy than the flat, straight traditional pods.

HISTORY

The name French bean was earned because the vegetable has long been a favourite in France, but the half-hardy plants originated in a warmer climate, perhaps in South America.

FOOD VALUE

Cooked beans provide Vitamin C, Vitamin A, mineral salts and dietary fibre.

SOWING AND PLANTING

A well-drained soil supplied with manure in winter and a sunny open site is needed for French beans. Outdoor sowings cannot be made until late spring as a minimum temperature of 50°F (10°C) is needed for germination. Sowings can be made from mid-spring under cloches if these are positioned 10 days earlier to warm the soil, or seed can be sown in deep trays or plant starters in a greenhouse in mid-spring, to transplant under cloches or into the open plot in late spring.

Sow seed a bare 2in (5cm) deep and 2-3in (5-8cm) apart with 18in (45cm) between rows. A midsummer sowing given cloche cover in early autumn will give young beans later in autumn.

AFTERCARE

French beans need ample water from flowering until harvest, and moisture around the roots can be conserved with a mulch. Pick every 2-3 days to ensure tender beans. Climbing varieties need supporting with posts and netting, or wires and strings.

PESTS AND DISEASES

Apart from slugs attacking newly germinated plants, there is usually little pest trouble. Grey mould (botrytis) can be a problem in wet seasons, and is best avoided by ensuring good ventilation around the plants. Other diseases should not be a problem if good seed is used and the rotation is followed.

Above: *For an early start raise French beans inside to transplant into the open (top). Gather pods regularly while young and tender.*

33

RUNNER BEANS

Runner beans are one of the most important vegetable crops. They can be harvested from mid-summer until mid-autumn to eat fresh or freeze for the cold months ahead. Most varieties are climbers, but you can grow dwarf forms for the earliest harvest.

HISTORY

A native of South America, the runner bean was brought to Europe in the 17th century. It was grown as a climbing plant for the beauty of scarlet blooms against lush green foliage for a very long time before anyone realized the value of the green pods for eating. Some modern varieties have pink or white blooms.

FOOD VALUE

Runner beans supply dietary fibre, mineral salts, some protein and some Vitamin A and Vitamin C.

SITE AND SOIL

An open sunny site with some shelter from strong wind is best for the crop. Runner beans respond well to liberal feeding and are best grown in a trench prepared in winter (see *Preparing the Ground,* page 14). Alternatively, dig a generous amount of rotted manure or garden compost into the strip of land intended for the crop.

Runner beans can safely be grown in one place for several years and so it can be worth installing posts and wires to hold up netting or string supports in the growing season.

CULTIVATION

Unlike the annual broad and French beans, runners are perennial if grown in a warm climate, and it is possible to save their thickened roots through winter as we do dahlia tubers, but it is far better to start anew from seed each year.

To ensure the longest possible season, stagger sowings, starting with seed sown under cloches in mid-spring, or in a deep tray or individual pots in the

Below: *Runner beans supported by tripods of canes can look very decorative (right). Alternatively the plants are allowed to climb up wires strung from crossed poles.*

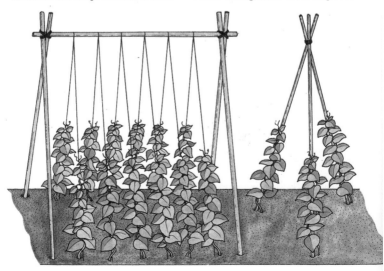

greenhouse or cold frame to be transplanted outside under cloches in mid to late spring; or sow seed in the open towards the end of spring.

Follow on with a succession of three sowings in the open at two-week intervals from the end of spring through early summer. One row containing four batches of plants will give a harvest over very much longer than the same row sown all at one time.

Before sowing or planting, work 2-3oz (50-70g) per sq yd (m) of general fertilizer into the site. There will be time for a catch crop of cloched lettuce and radish, or a first row of summer spinach, before the late runners need to go in.

SOWING AND PLANTING

Sow seed 2in (5cm) and 6in (15cm) apart in a double row 2ft (60cm) apart, or put in plants raised inside at the same spacing. They cannot go out unprotected until frost risk is past. The dwarf varieties are good for the earliest sowing under cloches and will give a crop of beans to pick very much quicker than a climbing variety of runner bean sown at the same time.

The early variety 'Kelvedon Marvel' can be kept low and bushy by pinching out climbing shoots. You can sow radish alongside the beans or put in plants of the dwarf 'Little Gem' lettuce to give a catch crop before the maincrop needs maximum space.

Climbing varieties must have sturdy supports at least 6ft (2m) high. Traditionally crossed poles or canes have been used, but now it is more usual to use posts, wires and netting or string; or to use a proprietary wigwam support.

Tall, handsome plants, runner beans can be used to form a decorative summer screen, or can be grown in groups up a tripod of canes as an ornamental feature at the back of a flower border. When they are used in this way, be very sure enough food and water is given.

AFTERCARE

Too much water in the early stages can lead to lush foliage at the expense of flowers, but from flowering on the plants need a lot of moisture. This can be conserved by applying a mulch along either side of the row.

It used to be thought that syringing the blooms with water would assist pod set, but now it is considered more important to grow plants well and pick very regularly so that no beans are allowed to mature, and new flowers are encouraged.

PESTS AND DISEASES

Slugs may be troublesome with newly germinated runner bean plants, but otherwise good strong plants fed and watered well are troubled by few pests or diseases.

Left: *The bean crop will be improved if a mulch of peat, or rotted organic matter, is spread along either side of the row to conserve moisture through summer. Apply when the soil is moist.*

BEETROOT

Beetroot is in season all year round: tender young roots in spring and summer, and stored maincrop in winter. You can pull your first round beet in late spring if you sow the modern bolt-resistant varieties under cloches, and follow on with the cylindrical and then the long type, which stores very well and has a superb flavour.

FOOD VALUE

The roots are a source of protein, carbohydrate, Vitamin C and dietary fibre. Although sometimes grated raw, they are usually cooked and have a much better colour and flavour when baked wrapped in foil than when boiled.

SITE AND SOIL

The crop is best grown on well-drained fertile land in an open sunny position, but should not be grown on a site that has recently been manured. Long varieties need a deep soil. In a three-year rotation, beetroot will be grown with the other roots on land manured the winter before last and used last summer for legumes, onions etc.

CULTIVATION

Ideally the ground should have been dug by mid-winter so that it is fairly easy to work down to a spring tilth. While this is being done 2-3oz (50-75g) of general fertilizer should be raked into the top few inches of each sq yd (m) of soil.

The earliest and latest beetroot can be regarded as catch crops to go in before or after a main planting, for they will occupy the site for only three months.

SOWING AND PLANTING

Sow seed of a bolt-resistant variety under cloches in early spring, on land where late brassicas will go in during mid-summer as the maincrop. Alternatively, sow seed in soil blocks in the greenhouse to transplant into the open or under cloches at 2in (5cm) high. A polytunnel cloche will give room for a row of beetroot and a broad drill of early carrots.

Except in a few varieties such as 'Monodet', each beetroot seed is really a cluster of several seeds within a cork-like pellet, and because of this it is important to sow thinly, aiming to sow 1in (2½cm) deep and apart in drills that are about 10in (25cm) apart.

Thin early beetroot to 1in (2½cm) apart and the maincrop to twice this distance, then use alternate roots for summer salads to give the others more room to develop. Thinnings can be transplanted to make another row when small if the weather is cool and showery.

Sow the first unprotected row in mid-spring, the maincrop in late spring, and an early variety in mid-summer to follow early peas and broad beans for sweet young autumn roots.

AFTERCARE

Early sowings in the open will probably need netting against birds. During routine weeding and

Below: *Globe beet have round roots and are the first to sow. The long type has always been considered best for storing. Cylindrical beet are midway between the two and economical of space.*

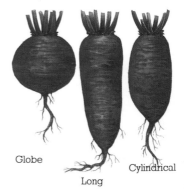

Globe

Long

Cylindrical

Above: *Twist the tops off beetroot, as cutting the leaf stalks may make the roots bleed (top). Store the roots for winter in boxes of very slightly damp sand, or peat, in a frost-free place.*

hoeing take care not to damage the tender beetroot skin as this can lead to bleeding. Water sufficiently through the season to maintain steady growth.

HARVESTING

Pull beetroot as needed, using the first round roots at golf ball size. Lift maincrop roots in mid-autumn before the first hard frost, rub off surplus soil, wring off the tops—cutting will cause bleeding and loss of colour from the roots—and store in boxes of slightly damp sand or peat in a frost-free dry place to bring indoors as needed through to late spring.

Store only good sound roots, putting aside any damaged specimens for early use. Inspect stored roots regularly and remove any that have started to rot. Surplus young summer roots can be cooked and frozen for winter use, or can be pickled in vinegar.

PESTS AND DISEASES

The crop is prone to boron and other mineral deficiences, but these should be no problem on soil regularly supplied with bulky organic material. Few diseases are likely to affect the crop. Birds and slugs are the main pests.

BROCCOLI

Essential for any well-stocked vegetable plot, purple and white sprouting broccolis are hardy enough to stand up to all but the severest winters. They yield succulent flowering shoots during the long weeks of spring when one has grown tired of winter cabbages and roots.

PURPLE, WHITE AND CALABRESE

The purple is hardier and a heavier cropper, but the white has a superior flavour. 'Nine Star Perennial' is an old broccoli that makes big plants with six to nine heads like miniature cauliflowers, and can be treated as a perennial where space is no object. But, as the best crop comes in the first year and older plants may carry over pests and diseases, it is better grown new from seed each year.

Calabrese green sprouting broccoli, with a central flower head surrounded by smaller sideshoots in early autumn, has a much shorter growing season and is not hardy. Its flavour has earned it the name 'poor man's asparagus'.

FOOD VALUE

All kinds of sprouting broccoli provide Vitamin C and other nutrients as well as dietary fibre. The tenderest small spears of white and purple are particularly nutritious when eaten raw in salads.

SITE AND SOIL

An open, sunny position on well-drained land is best for all forms of broccoli. Although the soil should be fertile, it does not want to be too rich, or white and purple varieties will make big, soft plants that will not come through winter well.

Calabrese in particular does not need such generous treatment as autumn cabbage and cauliflower.

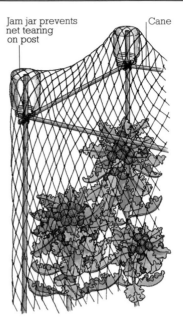

Jam jar prevents net tearing on post | Cane

Above: *Use net to protect spring-maturing broccoli from pigeons.*
Below: *Gather purple sprouting spears before the flowers open.*

CULTIVATION

Spring-cropping broccolis are raised in a seed bed in the open for transplanting in mid- to late summer to follow early vegetables. If the land has been treated well for these crops, no fertilizer will be needed at planting time, but if you feel some feeding is necessary give a dose of liquid feed with the first watering after planting. Calabrese can be transplanted, but is better sown in situ and thinned out.

SOWING AND PLANTING

Sow seed of the spring forms of sprouting broccoli in late spring, thinly in shallow drills, thinning where necessary to about 1in (2.5cm) apart and watering regularly to encourage quick growth and sturdy seedlings.

Below: *Cut the main head of calabrese first; this will make the smaller sideshoots develop for a later harvest.*

Harvest main flowerhead first

Feed to boost sideshoots

Transplant to 2-3ft (60-90cm) apart each way.

Calabrese can be sown at 3-4 weekly intervals from mid-spring to early summer, for a succession to harvest through late summer and early autumn. Spacings for this can be varied considerably, but it is hard to improve on 6in (15cm) between plants and 12in (30cm) between rows. Sow several seeds every 6in (15cm) along the row, later singling to one at each place.

AFTERCARE

Apart from early watering and routine hoeing and weeding, broccolis need little in the way of summer aftercare. In winter, tall plants in exposed gardens may need staking, and you will probably have to net against pigeons. At the end of winter, hoe in a top dressing of 1oz (25g) per sq yd (m) of a quick-acting nitrogenous fertilizer. Calabrese needs ample water all through the growing season.

HARVESTING

With all sprouting broccolis, it is important to pick shoots regularly immediately they are ready for the table, for once any stems have been allowed to actually flower, the plants will cease producing new shoots. With calabrese cut the first main flowerhead, give a dose of liquid feed to boost further growth, and then cut sideshoots as they develop.

PESTS AND DISEASES

There are few disease problems with broccoli. Cabbage root fly may affect transplants (see *Pests and Diseases* entry for cauliflower, page 46). Flea beetle may chew holes in seed leaves, but there is rarely serious damage. Caterpillars in calabrese can be controlled by spraying with fenitrothion or permethrin.

BRUSSELS SPROUTS

A favourite winter brassica, brussels sprouts will stand up to hard weather and can be harvested from September to March. In recent years, many F1 Hybrid varieties have been bred with a compact habit that allows closer spacing and suits them to the small garden.

HISTORY

Developed from the wild cabbage, *Brassica oleracea* that grows on sea cliffs on British and European coasts, brussels sprouts are believed to have originated in Belgium and were sold in markets there in the 13th century.

FOOD VALUE

Brussels sprouts are rich in Vitamin C, particularly when eaten raw, and are very good chopped and served in winter salads. They also contain significant amounts of Vitamin A, protein, carbohydrates and minerals, together with dietary fibre.

SITE AND SOIL

The plants do best in an open position on fertile land that has been deeply dug and supplied with ample humus, but not recently manured. Well-rotted garden compost worked in during the autumn is ideal.

Like all brassicas, brussels sprouts thrive in alkaline conditions, but they are prone to club root on acid soil. Here lime should be applied in the winter prior to planting.

Some shelter from strong winds is advisable, and tall varieties grown in an exposed position may need earthing up or staking.

CULTIVATION

Early brussels sprouts are planted in late spring, and the maincrop in early summer. This gives time to take a catch crop off the

Remove yellow leaves from late summer

Pick tight 'button' sprouts from base of stalk upwards

Pick 'blown' sprouts first

Above: *Having removed the loose 'blown' sprouts, pick the well-formed 'buttons' as needed. Use the tops for winter greens.*

site before they go in. Prepare the site for the sprouts by clearing weeds and all remains of the previous crop, working in 2oz (50g) of general fertilizer per sq yd (sq m), and, because they like firm soil, rolling or treading to consolidate the site where necessary.

SOWING AND PLANTING

Sow seed of early varieties under glass or polythene in very early spring, and of the maincrop two or three weeks later in the open. Sow thinly in shallow drills to allow room for seedlings to develop into sturdy plants, where necessary thinning seedlings to about 1in (2½cm) apart.

Transplant using a trowel so that the roots can be spread out, firming in each plant with the heel and filling the depression this makes in the soil with water.

Above: *As the buttons mature remove all the lower leaves from the plant to improve air circulation and allow easier picking. They can go on the compost heap. At the same time remove any diseased leaves and sprouts too loose for use in the kitchen.*

Dwarf varieties go in at 24in (60cm) and others at 30-36in (75-90cm) each way.

AFTERCARE

Give each newly transplanted sprout ¼pt (150ml) of water per day for the first three to four weeks in warm dry weather. After this they will need water only in really dry spells.

Some hand weeding and hoeing will be necessary in the early weeks, but once the plants have developed large leaves that almost cover the ground, little care is needed.

Firm planting is essential for brussels spouts. In exposed gardens and on lighter land draw some soil around the base of each stem in late summer to improve anchorage. From late summer onwards, yellowing lower leaves should be removed.

HARVESTING

Pick the tight 'button' sprouts from the base of the stalk upwards, first removing any lower ones that are loose and 'blown'. The cabbage-like tops of the plants are good to eat as winter greens.

PESTS AND DISEASES

Young seedlings may need netting to protect them from small birds and the mature plants from pigeons in late winter. Cabbage whitefly can be trapped if squares of wood painted deep yellow and coated with fruit tree grease, thinned with medicinal paraffin, are hung above the row. Avoid aphid problems by destroying over-wintered brassica plants by late spring. Handpick and destroy caterpillars. For cabbage root fly, see cauliflower (page 46).

CABBAGE

Plan your cabbage patch to give a steady succession of heads to cut all year, with a good choice of different kinds. There are varieties suited to all four seasons, and types with pointed or round heads and smooth or crinkled leaves in green, red and white.

HISTORY

Chinese cabbage is a brassica from the Orient that has been eaten there since at least the 5th century. All the other cabbages have come from the wild cabbage, *Brassica oleracea,* which is a native of British and European sea shores. They have been eaten since Roman times, and a 15th-century garden writer said that a succession could give heads to cut all year round.

FOOD VALUE

All cabbages are a source of Vitamin C, dietary fibre, mineral salts and other important nutrients and all but the winter white type contain Vitamin A. For greatest food value, eat freshly cut and raw, and when cooking steam in as little water as possible. Chinese cabbage provides Vitamin A, iron, calcium and other nutrients.

SITE AND SOIL

Cabbages need an open, unshaded site on fertile, well-drained and moisture-retentive land. Club root can be a problem where conditions are acid and to avoid this, lime is applied in the winter before planting. Ideally the site will have been winter dug and manured and then, for all but the summer varieties, used for early vegetables before the cabbages go in.

SOWING AND PLANTING

Summer cabbage: Sow seed in gentle heat in plant starters or soil blocks, for hardening off and transplanting into the open in early to mid-spring, or sow under cold glass at the same time for a slightly later planting in the open. Cloche cover in the first weeks outside will hasten growth.

These early varieties will not stand long before splitting. Follow them with a late summer/early autumn variety that will remain in good condition for some weeks, sowing seed in the open in early and mid-spring to transplant 5-6 weeks later. For all these, a spacing of 10-12in (25-30cm) each way is sufficient.
Red cabbage: Sow in the open in early and mid-spring to

Above: *Quick growing pointed heads of this F1 Hybrid are very compact, allowing close spacing.*

Above: *Red cabbages have been traditionally grown for pickling, but are good in autumn casseroles.*

transplant in late spring and early summer at 18in (45cm) each way, for heads to cut in autumn before hard frost comes to spoil them. These cabbages can be cut and stored on slatted shelves in a frost-free place for winter eating.

Remove loose outer leaves before storing, and inspect regularly for decaying leaves. Winter White cabbages are grown and stored in the same way.

Winter cabbage: This includes savoys with crinkled leaves, smooth-leaved drumheads and semi-savoys of the 'January King' type. Sow in mid-spring to transplant at 18-24in (45-60cm) each way, depending on variety, in early to mid-summer for cutting from mid- to late winter.

Grow several kinds for succession and a choice of eating. Cabbage seed remains viable for several years and so you will not need to buy each one every season. Work in 2oz (50g) per sq yd (m) of general fertilizer before planting.

Spring cabbage: Sow in mid- to late summer to transplant in early to mid-autumn in rows 12in (30cm) apart with 4in (10cm) between seedlings. In early spring, cut some for spring greens, leaving 12in (30cm) between plants that you want to make mature heads.

Chinese cabbage: This does not transplant well. Sow seed in mid- to late summer in drills 12in (30cm) apart with several seeds every 12in (30cm), later singling seedlings to one per station.

AFTERCARE

Weed, hoe and water as necessary for all types. When summer cabbage are established, give a dose of liquid feed. Chinese cabbage must have plenty of water, and will not stand hard frost. Cloche cover from mid-autumn will extend the season.

In cold districts, overwinter spring cabbage under cloches. Uncovered plants may need netting or other protection from birds. In late winter give them 1-2oz (25-50g) per sq yd (m) of quick-acting nitrogenous fertilizer to hasten development.

PESTS AND DISEASES

Few diseases affect cabbage other than those dealt with in the general *Pests and Diseases* section (page 26). For cabbage root fly, see *Pests and Diseases* entry for cauliflowers, page 46. Handpick and destroy caterpillars. Avoid aphis trouble by destroying old, overwintered brassica plants by late spring.

Above: *Savoy cabbages with crinkled leaves have a better flavour after some frost.*

Above: *Chinese cabbage mature to tight pale heads that are good to eat raw in autumn salads.*

CARROTS

In season all year, very nutritious, good to eat raw or cooked, and easy on space in the garden, carrots are a must for every culinary plot. Modern varieties have been bred for a deeper orange colour, for better texture and quality.

HISTORY

Developed from the wild carrot that grows in many parts of Europe, the vegetable was mentioned in a book written 500 years ago. One published in 1548 tells us that carrots grew in all countries in plenty.

FOOD VALUE

The roots are valued for their high Vitamin A content that helps improve sight in the dark. They are also high in Vitamin C and contain dietary fibre, mineral salts and trace elements.

SITE AND SOIL

A warm, sheltered place is best for the early crop, but a more open site for the maincrop.

Carrots do best on well-drained, light and fertile soil, and are difficult to grow well on heavy clay and other soils that dry out hard and rocky, or contain many stones.

To improve structure, the land should be deeply dug and regularly supplied with bulky organic material, although recently manured land will lead to forked roots of little use in the kitchen.

CULTIVATION

Carrots are a good crop to follow autumn and mid-winter brassicas. These can be cleared in time for land to be dug and left for frosty weather to help the topsoil crumble down into a fine tilth. A week or so before sowing, 2-3oz (50-75g) of general fertilizer should be raked into every sq yd (m) of land.

Below: *For economy of space sow carrots in broad shallow drills the width of a hoe blade. Thin when the soil is moist, or water the row a few hours beforehand. To help avoid root fly do the job in the evening.*

Above: *Carrots sown in early summer can be pulled quite small in late summer to go in the deep freeze, leaving the ground free for another crop, or can be left to grow on to make larger roots to store in boxes of sand.*

SOWING

Carrots are grown from seed to harvest in one place. For the earliest harvest sow in a frame, or under cloches that have been in position for 10-14 days to warm the soil, in late winter/early spring providing the weather is not too cold. Sow the early unprotected crop in early to mid-spring.

Maincrop sowings are best delayed until summer has begun, to avoid trouble from the first batch of carrot root fly. These roots can all be pulled at finger-size in late summer to freeze—a particularly good plan where root fly is prevalent—or grown on to make large roots for storing.

Traditionally carrots have been grown in narrow drills, spaced at about 12in (30cm) apart, but recent research has shown that better use is made of land if they are grown in blocks of short rows at about half this distance apart. Another method is to grow them in broad drills made with the width of the hoe blade to give a band of carrots 4-6in (10-15cm) wide across the plot.

Drills should be a good ½in (1·5cm) deep, and seed should be sown thinly to avoid a lot of thinning. This applies especially to the maincrop, which germinates better than early sowings because the soil is warmer.

AFTERCARE

Water the row before and after you thin the carrots, or pull for the table, and do the job in the evening to cut down risk of attack by root fly. Maincrop plants will need thinning to 2in (5cm) apart. Slightly earth up the plants during routine hoeing to prevent green tops, caused by exposure to light. Water sufficiently to maintain steady growth, as an erratic water supply leads to split roots.

HARVESTING

Pull young roots as needed. Lift the maincrop in early to mid-autumn with a fork, taking care not to spear the roots. Twist off the tops and rub off surplus soil, or wash with the hose, so that you can detect any damaged carrots. Put these aside for early eating and store sound roots in boxes of slightly damp sand, or peat, in a frost-free place.

PESTS AND DISEASES

Root fly maggots which eat the roots are the main pest. They are warded off by following the cultural methods advised above; otherwise, control with Bromophos, dusted into the seed drills before sowing and sprinkled along the row after thinning. Rotation of crops, good growing and garden hygiene should prevent most other troubles.

CAULIFLOWER

Cauliflowers can be harvested from late winter to late autumn, but few gardeners are able to produce a succession through all this time. The most welcome are those ready to cut in early to late spring, but they occupy the ground for many months and may be killed by a hard winter.

HISTORY

Cauliflowers originated in the Mediterranean region and have been grown in Europe for at least 400 years, but they have been cultivated on a wide scale only since the 18th century.

FOOD VALUE

They are rich in potassium and contain protein, phosphorus, Vitamin C and dietary fibre.

SOWING AND PLANTING

Deeply dug, fertile and moisture-retentive soil not deficient in lime is necessary. It is important to avoid any check to growth, particularly at transplanting time, and for this reason earlier varieties should be raised inside in soil blocks or individual pots, and transplanted in about six weeks from sowing. Work in 4oz (100g) per sq yd (m) of general fertilizer before planting.

Early summer cauliflowers: Sow in mid-autumn in a cold frame, or in gentle heat in late winter to transplant in early spring at 21in (52cm) each way.

Mini cauliflowers: Sow *in situ* in succession from mid-spring to mid-summer at 6in (15cm) each way, putting in several seeds to thin to one per station, for tiny curds ideal for freezing.

Late summer: Sow under cold glass in early spring, then in the open for succession. Transplant after six weeks at 21in (52cm) each way .

Autumn: Sow in open in late spring to plant in mid-summer at 21in (52cm) each way for

Above: *Bend a leaf over to protect the maturing cauliflower curd from the sun and rain.*
Below: *Harvest when curds are a good size, firm and white.*

Australian varieties, 27in (67cm) each way for others.

Spring: Sow in late spring/early summer to transplant in mid-summer at 24-30in (60-75cm) each way, choosing several varieties for a succession from early to late spring. Top dress with quick-acting nitrogenous fertilizer in late winter.

PESTS AND DISEASES

To avoid cabbage root fly trouble with cauliflowers put in during summer, surround each transplant with a 6in (15cm) disc of foam carpet underlay. For caterpillar control see broccoli (page 39).

CELERY

Traditionally, celery has been grown in a trench and earthed up to blanch the leaf stalks. Nowadays more people grow the self-blanching varieties, whose heads are however seldom of a quality to match well-grown trench varieties. A rarer crop is the turnip-rooted type of celery, called celeriac.

HISTORY

All the celeries are descended from smallage, a wild flower of the parsley/carrot family. Some gardeners bred for leaf stalk, while others selected swollen, bulb-like stems, producing the two crops now known as celery and celeriac.

FOOD VALUE

Celery provides mineral salts, Vitamin C and dietary fibre, while celeriac gives these plus significant amounts of potassium, trace elements and some protein.

SITE AND SOIL

Lovers of marshland, all the celeries grow best on moisture-retentive, fertile soil, rich in organic matter, in an open, sunny position, and do not like acid conditions.

CULTIVATION

Celery and celeriac are half-hardies to start inside, for transplanting into the open when frost is past. For self-blanching (S-B) celery and celeriac, deep digging and generous applications of bulky organic manures, in the winter before planting, are advisable.

Blanched celery is grown in a trench, prepared in winter. (See *Preparing the Ground,* page 14).

SOWING AND PLANTING

Sow S-B celery in early to mid-spring, trench varieties and celeriac in mid-spring. Sow thinly in pans, with very little covering compost, at a temperature of 10-15°C (50-60°F). Prick out seedlings when the first true leaves appear, with five to a planting strip, or into individual soil blocks. Grow on under cold glass to harden off well before planting. Take care to label,

Below: *Plant traditional varieties of celery in two staggered rows, in a trench dug out in winter and part-filled with rotted organic matter. Wrap the plants in brown paper late in summer and then surround them with topsoil to protect them from frost and blanch them.*

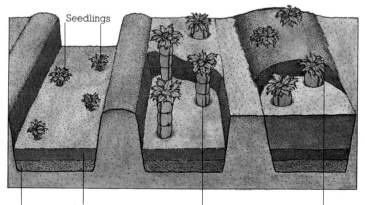

Seedlings

3in (7.5cm) manure

3in (7.5cm) topsoil

Brown paper tied round stem

Topsoil

CELERY

Above: *Self-blanching celery is planted in a block of short rows on the flat in fertile soil.*

Above: *From mid-summer on remove sideshoots and lower leaves to expose celeriac crowns.*

as the different types are very hard to tell apart.

Rake 1oz (25g) per sq yd (m) of quick-acting nitrogenous fertilizer into the site before planting any of the celeries, and water well afterwards.

S-B celery can be planted in an empty cold frame in late spring to grow on until harvest, but it is more often planted in very late spring in the open, in a block of short rows with seedlings at 9-11in (22-28cm) apart each way.

Celeriac is also grown on the flat, but needs spacing at 12-15in (30-37cm) each way.

Trench celery is planted in early summer, with a double row of plants at 10in (25cm) each way. When seedlings are grown in planting strips or blocks, watered a few hours before the move, there is very little root disturbance.

AFTERCARE

Generous watering is needed all season, and the plants benefit from regular liquid feeding. Keep the site weed free. In mid- to late summer remove old outer leaves from celeriac to expose the crown and improve quality. Protect with straw in frosty

weather. Celeriac can be stored, but quality deteriorates in store.

S-B celery blocks should be surrounded with straw or black polythene sheet, to blanch the outer heads, during late summer.

Trench celery is earthed up from late summer onwards, choosing a time when the soil is damp but plants are dry. This entails three operations: first remove outer, yellowing leaves and sideshoots; then wrap each plant in a collar made from corrugated, or stout brown, paper tied at top and bottom; finally draw up soil to near the base of the leaves.

Well-earthed celery will stand up to quite hard frost, so this traditional form has a longer season than the S-B varieties.

PESTS AND DISEASES

Slugs are a big problem with celery, particularly the trenched crop, and leads to heart rot.

Thiram-treated seed is protected from leaf spot disease. Avoid planting seedlings with leaves blistered by celery fly and remove any blistered foliage that you discover during growth.

Carrot fly affects mainly celeriac and where this is prevalent the crop is inadvisable.

CUCUMBER

Outdoor cucumbers used to be very poor relations of the elegant greenhouse varieties, with short, tubby fruits that had bumpy skins and often hard seeds and a bitter taste. These old outdoor varieties cannot compare with the new outdoor F1 Hybrids, which produce longer, smoother fruit of superb quality.

FOOD VALUE

The fruits supply Vitamin C, folic acid, mineral salts and, if eaten with the skin, dietary fibre.

SITE AND SOIL

Cucumbers need good drainage, but really fertile and moisture-retentive land in a warm site sheltered from stong winds. Outdoor varieties used to be referred to as ridge cucumbers and it was usual to grow them on slightly raised mounds to assist drainage. This can still be done, but it is more usual to grow them on the flat.

On poorer land it is best to prepare individual stations for the plants by digging out holes 12in (30cm) deep and about 18in (45cm) square, working a thick layer of rotted manure or garden compost into the bottom and then replacing the soil, leaving a slightly raised mound on heavy land.

An easier method, and one that works well on fertile soil, is to dig in a generous amount of rotted organic matter during the winter before planting. Work 1oz (25g) per sq yd (m) of quick-acting nitrogenous fertilizer into the site before sowing or planting.

Left: *For quality fruit and economy of space train outdoor cucumber plants up netting or canes.*
Below: *Providing cloche cover for the first weeks will given an early harvest of outdoor cucumbers.*

CUCUMBER

CULTIVATION

Outdoor cucumbers can be sown *in situ* and grown completely in the open, but as they are half-hardy they cannot be sown outside before late spring, and this gives a late harvest and a short season. It is far better to start plants in gentle heat indoors.

Growth can be speeded up further if they are protected in the first weeks outdoors with cloches or individual night covers.

The plants can be grown on the flat, with stems trailing over the ground, and make a good intercrop among sweet corn. But, for economy of space and to ensure straight high quality fruit, train the stems up netting.

Cucumbers can be grown from planting throughout the rest of the season under larger cloches or in a frame.

SOWING AND PLANTING

Sow seed on edge in individual 3in (8cm) pots of potting compost in mid- to late spring in a temperature of 15°C (60°F)—perhaps on a windowsill indoors; or buy pre-germinated plantlets ready to prick out into pots. Move them to a cooler place once the seed leaves have fully expanded, and grow on under cold glass until at least one pair of true leaves has formed.

3in (7.5cm) pots
Moist seed compost

Above: *Start outdoor cucumbers indoors and grow on in pots to plant out when frost risk is past.*

Above: *Pinch out the growing tips of cucumber plants after five or six true leaves have formed to encourage bushy growth.*

The plants will not stand frost and cannot go out into the open until mid- to late spring, but can be planted outdoors at this time if given some protection. Put them in 18in (45cm) apart if they are to climb, or 24in (60cm) apart if they are to trail over the ground.

AFTERCARE

Regular watering is needed throughout the season except in wet weather and liquid feeding from the time that the first fruits begin to grow out, except on very fertile land. It is not necessary to remove male flowers from outdoor cucumbers.

A mulch of black polythene sheet raises soil temperature, keeps down weeds, and keeps fruit on the ground clean and free from the rot that can occur in wet weather. Pick cucumbers regularly a little before they reach maximum size for best quality, and to encourage plants to go on producing flowers.

PESTS AND DISEASES

Trouble from slugs and woodlice at the succulent seed leaf stage can be largely avoided by growing the plants inside, in pots. Avoid powdery mildew on those growing in frames or under cloches by good ventilation.

KALE

Kale is the hardiest brassica and particularly valuable for growing in colder areas. There are plain-leaved and curly forms, and 'Pentland Brig' is a hybrid between the two. Ornamental kales are grown, too: these have frilly purple, white and green leaves, and are nice to eat as well as to look at.

HISTORY

Developed from the wild cabbage, this once functioned as a staple food in parts of Scotland, where the main meal of the day came to be known as kale.

FOOD VALUE

This is a good source of Vitamin C and contains also Vitamin A and a certain amount of mineral salts and trace elements.

SITE AND SOIL

Kale will thrive on poorer land and in more acid conditions than most brassicas, but does best on well-cultivated fertile soil in a sunny open position. It is a good follow-on crop to early peas and beans on land manured and deeply dug the previous autumn.

SOWING AND PLANTING

Sow seed in shallow drills in the open in mid- to late spring to transplant in mid- to late summer, with dwarf forms at 15-18in (37-45cm) each way and taller kinds at 24in (60cm) each way, planting firmly with the lower leaves just above soil level.

AFTERCARE AND HARVESTING

Earth up the stems of taller plants in autumn to prevent winds rocking them loose. Top dress with 1oz (25g) per sq yd (m) of quick-acting nitrogenous fertilizer in late winter. Flavour is improved by frost, and kale is in season from late autumn to mid-spring. When harvesting, cut the younger leaves and sideshoots and avoid older coarse foliage.

PESTS AND DISEASES

The crop is not greatly affected by pests or diseases, though it may need protecting from pigeons in winter. See brussels sprouts (page 41) for whitefly, broccoli (page 39) for caterpillars, and cabbages (page 43) for aphis treatment.

Below: *Cut younger leaves and sideshoots from curly kale as needed from late autumn through to spring. Older foliage will be too coarse and strongly-flavoured for good eating.*

LEEKS

One of the hardiest vegetables, the leek is a good standby for eating right through winter and is particularly valuable for those living in colder districts. The plants occupy the land for a long time, but remain in good condition despite this.

FOOD VALUE

The vegetable contains Vitamin C, protein, mineral salts and dietary fibre.

SITE AND SOIL

Leeks grow best in fertile, well-drained soil in an open position. Grow them on land deeply dug and manured during the winter before planting. Plants are raised in a seedbed for transplanting in early to mid-summer, and so the crop can be grown as a follow-on to early lettuce, peas or broad beans.

SOWING AND PLANTING

Seed can be sown in the open in early spring, but for the early crop sow under cloches or in a frame in late winter and early spring. An even earlier start comes from sowing in a pan in gentle heat, then pricking out the seedlings at 1½in (4cm) each way under cold glass to grow on until pencil-thick and about 8in (20cm) high.

Rake 1oz (25g) per sq yd (m) of quick-acting nitrogenous fertilizer into the site before planting. Planting is easier if the tops of the leaves and the bottoms of the fibrous roots are cut off. Make holes 6in (15cm) deep and the same distance apart in rows 12in (30cm) apart with a dibber, drop a plant in each one, water well with the can minus its rose, but do not replace the soil.

AFTERCARE

Water regularly until the plants are established, and again in dry spells through the rest of summer. Drawing up soil around the base of the plants two or three times in autumn, until only the tops of the leaves are visible, gives long blanched stems. Dig leeks as needed from late autumn to spring.

Above: *Newly planted leeks will need watering regularly until new roots have formed.*

Above: *Lift leeks as needed through the cold months. The green tops can be used in soups.*

LETTUCE

Lettuce is one of the most important crops for the vegetable plot, for the leaves lose quality quickly after cutting, but are much nicer and more nutritious if eaten really fresh.

FOOD VALUE

The leaves provide potassium and other mineral salts, some protein and dietary fibre, trace elements and Vitamins A and C.

SITE AND SOIL

Aim for an open, sunny site on light, fertile, moisture-retentive soil. Adequate moisture is very important during summer, but beware of overhead irrigation as water may collect among the leaves and lead to rotting.

Grow lettuce on land that has been supplied with bulky organic material in winter, fitting in the quick-growing plants as a catch crop before a main planting or as an intercrop.

Work 2oz (50g) of general fertilizer per sq yd (m) into the site before planting. At both ends of the season lettuce is a top priority for space under cloches or in a frame.

CULTIVATION

Start a first batch of lettuce by sowing seed in gentle heat, perhaps on a windowsill indoors, in mid-winter, choosing a variety from the successional chart. Follow on with a sowing under cold glass or plastic and then make successional sowings in the open every three weeks from early spring to late summer.

Thin adequately to allow ample room for full development and for a good air circulation, allowing 5-6in (13-15cm) each way between dwarf cos and loose leaf, twice this distance between the larger cos and early butterheads, and 12in (30cm) each way between the larger summer butterheads and crispheads.

A good new method for an early crop under cover is leaf lettuce produced by sowing a cos variety in a block of short drills 5in (13cm) apart, thinning to 1in (2.5cm) apart and then gathering leaves from the time they are about 3in (8cm) high.

Above: *Lettuce seedlings planted in a block at equal distances each way—a method which is particularly appropriate for an early or late crop of lettuce grown under cover in a cold frame.*

LETTUCE

SOWING AND PLANTING

Sowing direct into plant starters or soil blocks, or pricking out into these as soon as the seed leaves have fully expanded, minimizes root disturbance at planting time and cuts down the growing time required by the early plants raised inside. Sow thinly in shallow drills through the warmer months, aiming for 20 plants from each batch.

Lettuce does not germinate well in hot weather and at mid-summer it is best to sow late in the day so that the critical period is passed during the night, and to soak the bottom of the drill with cold water before putting in the seed. The loose-leaf type that is gathered leaf by leaf is specially good for late summer.

Traditionally the first spring lettuce have come from plants grown from a mid-autumn sowing to overwinter in the open or under cloches, but they may not survive a hard winter, and seedlings started indoors to go out under cloches will be ready to cut almost as soon.

PESTS AND DISEASES

Greenfly is at its worst in dry springs, or when plants are grown near trees. An aluminium-foil mulch helps prevent the aphids from alighting.

Above: *Cos lettuce sown in early autumn and overwintered in the open for spring cutting.*

A LETTUCE SUCCESSION	
Varieties	**Type**
EARLY SOWINGS UNDER GLASS	
Fortune	But
Hilde 11	But
Suzan	But
Kellys	Cr
OUTDOOR SOWINGS FOR SUMMER	
Avondefiance	But
Barcarolle	Cos
Buttercrunch	Dw Cos
Dolly	But
Lake Nyah	Cr
Little Gem	Dw Cos
Minetto	Cr
Sabine	But
Salad Bowl	L
Saladin	Cr
Sigmahead	But
OUTDOOR OVERWINTERING CROP	
Arctic King	But
Valdor	But
Winter Density	Cos
PROTECTED CROP FOR LATE AND EARLY SEASON	
Kwiek	But
Note: The numbers refer to calendar months in a normal 'mild' year in southern England.	

Sg	Sc	S	Pc	P	Cl	Hc	H
1-3	2-3		2-4	4		4-5	6
1-3	2-3		2-4	4		4-5	6
1-3	2-3		2-4	4		4-5	6
1-3	2-3		2-4	4		4-5	6
		6-8		7-8		9-11	8-10
		3-6		4-7			6-9
	3	3-7		4-7			6-9
	2-3	3-4	3-4	4-5		5-6	6-7
		3-6		4-7			6-9
	3-4	3-7	4	4-8		6	6-10
		3-6		4-7			6-9
		6-8		7-9		9-11	8-10
		6-8					8-11
		3-6		4-7			6-9
		3-7		4-8			6-10
	10	9	10-12	10	10-12	3-4	4-5
	10	9	10-12	10	10-12	3-4	4-5
	10	9	10-12	10	10-12	3-4	4-5
	8-10	8-10	10-12		10-12	11-12	3-4

Key: But—Butterhead, Cr—Crisphead, Dw—dwarf, L—Looseleaf, 1-12—Jan-Dec, **Sg**—sow in gentle heat, **Sc**—sow under cold glass, **S**—sow in open, **Pc**—plant under cold glass, **P**—plant in open, **Cl**—cover with cloches, **Hc**—harvest under cover, **H**—harvest in open.

MARROWS, COURGETTES AND PUMPKINS

The marrow used to be a favourite cottage garden crop, but today many people have gone over to growing courgettes. These are baby marrows, and if not cut young will grow into the familiar stripey big fruits. Marrows and courgettes are close relatives of the pumpkin.

HISTORY

Courgettes take their name from the French and one variety carries the Italian name *zucchini*. Probably of South American origin, marrows are thought to have come to Europe early last century and soon became very popular.

Pumpkins were grown by the South American Indians of old, have been cultivated in Europe since at least the 16th century and were popular in the 17th century for pies.

FOOD VALUE

All three vegetables contain some Vitamin A and C, mineral salts and trace elements, although a very large percentage of the contents is water.

SITE AND SOIL

An open sunny site on moisture-retentive, but well-drained, soil that is very rich in organic matter is best for the marrow family. It is usual to prepare individual stations (see cucumbers, page 49), but when a very generous amount of rotted manure or garden compost has been dug into the land in winter there is no need to do this. Fork over the ground before planting, working in 1oz (25g) of quick-acting nitrogenous fertilizer per sq yd (m).

CULTIVATION

These are half-hardy vegetables that cannot be sown *in situ* until late spring. That will give a

Above: *Bush marrow plants with exotic yellow blooms are showy enough to plant in the decorative parts of the garden.*

crop, but to produce marrows and courgettes early on while shop prices are high and achieve a good yield throughout the season you need to start plants inside. This also helps protect seedlings from slugs at the vulnerable seed leaf stage.

While all courgettes grow into marrows, not all varieties of marrow can be used as courgettes, but only those with long slim fruits. Shorter plumper varieties and those with round or top-shaped fruits are not suitable. Courgettes and similar marrows are grown on bush plants. Some marrows, and the pumpkin, come on trailing plants whose stems will romp over the ground: these can sometimes be trained up netting.

SOWING AND PLANTING

Sow from mid-spring in individual 3in (8cm) pots of potting compost in gentle heat or in a cold greenhouse, growing on to harden off and plant into the open

Above: *Cut courgettes every two or three days while small, or they will develop into big marrows. The plants need plenty of water.*

Above: *Pumpkins grow on trailing plants and need plenty of room. Allow them to mature on the plants, but cut to store before frost.*

garden after about four weeks when two or more true leaves will have developed. None of the marrow family can be planted completely into the open until frost risk is past, but they can go out in late spring if covered with glass or plastic at night and on cold days during the following three or four weeks.

Bush varieties and trailers that are to be trained up netting need to go in 3ft (1m) apart, and those that will trail over the ground at 4ft (1·5m) apart. To use continuous cloches would be a waste, and it's better to use individual covers (see cucumbers, page 50) for protection.

Sow radish seed thinly in a ring around marrows and courgettes immediately after planting, and you will have pulled their plump red roots for salad before the main vegetables need anything like all their space. Well-grown marrows and courgettes crop so well that three or four plants will produce enough for the average household.

AFTERCARE

All the marrow family need copious water throughout the season unless the weather is rainy. Surrounding plants with a mulch of lawn mowings or black polythene sheeting cuts down on weeding, conserves moisture and keeps the fruit clean. Harvest regularly at either the baby courgette or marrow size to encourage more flowers.

For large pumpkins allow no more than two or three fruits to develop on each plant. Cut ripe marrows and pumpkins for store before the first frost is expected and hang in nets in a frost-free place. The crop benefits from liquid feeding from the time the fruits begin to swell.

PESTS AND DISEASES

Apart from slug trouble soon after germination, well-grown plants of the marrow family are not usually much affected by pests or diseases.

ONIONS

Frequently needed in the kitchen, onions are not at all difficult to grow well and can be brought in fresh from the garden, or from store, through most of the year. Shallots are an easy crop that costs little to produce, because bulbs for planting are saved from the previous season's harvest.

HISTORY

Onions have a very long history, were eaten in ancient India and China and by the workmen building the Pyramids in Egypt. In the early Middle Ages they were an important vegetable to eat in winter when fresh green foodstuffs were scarce.

FOOD VALUE

Onions have long been valued for health-giving properties and are thought to help ward off colds. They provide potassium, calcium and other mineral and trace elements, as well as some Vitamin C and dietary fibre.

SITE AND SOIL

Choose an open sunny position on fertile, well-drained soil for the onion bed. It should ideally be double dug with plenty of well-rotted manure or garden compost worked into the lower spit in the autumn before sowing or planting. Rake in 2oz (50g) per sq yd (m) of general fertilizer during preparation of the site.

GROWING FROM SEED

Sow onion seed thinly for the maincrop in early spring in shallow drills 12in (30cm) apart and thin seedlings to 2-3in (5-8cm) apart depending on whether you are aiming for medium-sized or large bulbs. Pickling varieties go in at the same time. These are sown more thickly in a broad drill, made with the width of the hoe blade, 5-7in (13-17cm) wide. They are not thinned, as the aim is for small bulbs crowded together.

Older varieties, sown in late summer, are thinned to only 1in (2.5cm) apart in autumn and to the final spacing in spring. If they are sown indoors, sowing is at mid-winter, in pans at a temperature of 61°F (16°C), and planting out is in early spring.

Earliest of the new season's onions are the modern Japanese varieties, which are sown out-

doors in late summer and mature very early next summer. But these require considerable skill to grow.

GROWING FROM SETS

Onion sets are partly developed bulbs that grow very rapidly after they are planted. If you buy heat-treated onion sets, delay planting these until early to mid-spring to avoid bolting. Choose small sets of no more than ¾in (2cm) diameter, because they are less likely to bolt and there are more to the pound (kilo).

Snip off dried tops to prevent birds or earthworms pulling up the sets, and push them firmly into the ground so only tips show, at 2-4in (5-10cm) apart, depending on the size of bulb required, with 10in (25cm) between rows.

Also available are autumn sets,

Above: *Japanese onions from a late summer seed sowing are grown close enough for the bulbs to touch one another at maturity.*
Left: *Larger bulbs result from a wider spacing. On poorer land liquid feed every couple of weeks from when the onions start to swell. Keep the bed weed-free.*

Top: *Clusters of shallots are ready to lift and dry off as soon as tops turn brown and die down.*
Above: *Like shallots, ripe onions are lifted carefully with a fork and dried off for ten days or so before storing. Drying is assisted in a bad season if they are laid out under cloches.*

best planted in early to mid-autumn, which will give mature bulbs in early summer.

Shallot bulbs are planted in late winter to mid-spring, 6in (15cm) apart with 8in (20cm) between the rows.

AFTERCARE

Keep the onion bed weed free. Water regularly in dry spells, until mid-summer (see *Watering*, page 22), giving special attention to newly-planted seedlings. Liquid feed on poorer land, and for big bulbs, once the onions have started to swell out. Autumn sown or planted onions should be given a top dressing of 1-2oz (25-50g) per sq yd (m) of quick-acting nitrogenous fertilizer in late winter.

HARVESTING

Lift onions once their tops have turned yellow and died down. Spread them out to dry on netting, or make use of an empty frame or cloches to assist drying in a wet season. Put damaged bulbs aside for early use and store sound onions in bunches, ropes, or spread out on slatted trays.

Above: *A rope of ripe onions ready to store in a frost-free place for use as needed during winter.*

Lift shallots once the tops have died down and spread them out to dry on fine netting. Once they are really dry, rub off loose skins and store in nets, putting aside enough medium-sized bulbs for the following spring's planting.

PEST AND DISEASES

Avoid white rot of the onion base by thinning in good time, rotating crops and not growing on affected land; avoid neck rot by storing only sound bulbs, inspecting those in store regularly and removing any affected onions. Prevent trouble from stem and bulb eelworm, which causes swollen distorted leaves and split bulbs, by rotating crops and good weed control; prevent both onion fly and bean seed fly—the maggots feed in the bulbs—by sowing late summer seeds into a 'stale' seed bed that has been prepared for ten days.

Above: *To make a rope of onions, knot the ends of a 3ft (90cm) length of string and tie the leaves of the first onion through the loop. Weave the second onion into the string so it rests on the first, tighten and repeat.*

PARSNIPS

One of the easiest crops to grow, parsnips can be dug from the garden as needed right through winter. Modern canker-resistant varieties have dumpy roots with wide fleshy shoulders and are not only easier to grow but also much nicer to eat than the older types.

FOOD VALUE

Parsnips contain dietary fibre, some potassium, calcium and other mineral salts and trace elements, and Vitamins C and E.

SOWING AND PLANTING

An open site on light, deep and well-cultivated land that is not deficient in lime is best, but the crop will grow on most soils, though stony ground should be avoided when possible. Never grow on a newly-manured site, as this leads to forked roots. Rake the soil down to a fine tilth, working in 2oz (50g) per sq yd (m) of general fertilizer before sowing. This used to be done in late winter, but now early to mid-spring sowing has been found to give better results.

Parsnip seed has a short life, so you must buy new each season. A spacing of 3in (8cm) apart, with 8-10in (20-25cm) between rows gives roots of a good size. Sow several seeds at this spacing along the drill, to thin to one per station at 2in (5cm) high.

Germination is slow and a sprinkling of radish seed in the same drill will provide row markers and a catch crop before the parsnips need thinning.

Little care is needed through summer, apart from weeding in the early stages and watering enough to maintain steady growth. When the foliage dies down in autumn, mark the rows so you will know where to dig for roots. These can be lifted and stored for a short time, but are better freshly dug. The flavour of parsnips is better after a sharp frost.

PESTS AND DISEASES

Avoid canker by growing a resistant variety and not sowing until early to mid-spring. See carrots (page 45) for root fly treatment.

Below: *Grown at the modern close spacing, parsnips give a higher yield of well-shaped roots of a good size for eating.*

PEAS

It is a challenge to grow them well and defend them from pests, but you can produce peas from late spring through to autumn to eat raw in salads, cook while they are really young, or stock the freezer. Most people go for dwarf types, but for the highest yield you cannot equal the older, tall maincrop varieties.

HISTORY

One of the earliest vegetables grown by man, the pea was eaten in Europe during the Stone Age and in Asia nearly 10,000 years BC. Dried peas were an important part of the winter diet during the Middle Ages.

FOOD VALUE

Fresh or frozen peas provide Vitamins A and C and some B6, protein, dietary fibre, mineral salts, and trace elements.

SITE AND SOIL

Choose a site that is open but not too exposed, and deeply dug fertile soil that was manured in the autumn before planting, and is both well-drained and moisture-retentive. On really good land no fertilizer should be necessary, but on poorer soil work in 2oz (50g) per sq yd (m) before sowing.

CULTIVATION

In milder sheltered areas the hardier round-seeded peas can be sown in mid- to late autumn, preferably under cloche cover, for a late spring harvest. These varieties can also be sown in late winter under cloches, but it is better to wait until very early spring for the first sowing of the better-flavoured wrinkled peas under cloches, and they should not go into open ground until two or three weeks later.

Second early varieties can be sown from mid-spring, and if you put in a row of them at the

Top left: *Sugar peas, supported by sticks in the traditional manner.*
Left: *Peas supported by netting and stakes on each side of the row.*
Top right: *The asparagus pea, with its curious winged pods.*
Above: *An open pod of peas at just the right age for picking.*

same time as a row of the tall maincrops one will follow the other for a succession after the cloched row.

Peas can be sown for a further succession through to early/mid-summer with a final row of the first early 'Kelvedon Wonder' going in during mid-summer for new peas in autumn, but it is the early rows that are most important, for they give a harvest before the wide choice of late summer vegetables. Mange-tout or sugar peas are sown from early spring to early summer.

Although usually sown *in situ*, early peas can be raised in planting strips or soil blocks to plant out under cloches, or in the open. This saves time in a

late spring and gives protection from birds, mice and slugs in the first very vulnerable stages.

SOWING AND PLANTING

Peas can be sown in single lines, but are more often sown in broad drills made with the width of the hoe, about 8in (20cm) wide and 1½in (4cm) deep, and with three lines of seed at 3in (8cm) each way in the row.

A new technique is to grow them in deep beds about 3ft (1m) wide with seeds 2-3in (5-8cm) apart all over: for this use a leafless, self-supporting variety with many tendrils, such as 'Poppet'.

Most peas need supporting from an early age with twiggy sticks saved from pruning, wire netting, or plastic bean netting supported by tall stakes.

AFTERCARE

Mulch the pea row with lawn mowings (that have not been treated with weedkiller) to conserve moisture, and water generously from flowering to harvest to improve yield. Keep weeds down. Gather pods regularly while the peas are young, because they are nicest then and this encourages the plants to go on cropping. Sugar peas are best picked at about 3in (8cm) long when peas are just beginning to swell the fleshy pods.

PESTS AND DISEASES

Protect seeds from mice by soaking in paraffin before sowing, or putting down traps by the early row under cloches or netting pea guards. Protect young seedlings and developing pods from birds with netting, or plastic humming line scarers. To avoid pea moth maggots grow only early peas, or spray 7-10 days after the first flowers with fenitrothion. Use this, too, against the thrips that distort blooms and leave silver markings on the pods.

POTATOES

In a small garden it is not worth growing maincrop potatoes, for they take up a lot of room both to grow and store. But you should give priority to a row of a first early variety, for new potatoes are much nicer and more nutritious eaten soon after digging.

HISTORY

Enjoyed by the Incas of South America for 2,000 years, potatoes did not come to Europe until the 16th century and were at first considered a novelty rather than an important crop.

FOOD VALUE

Young fresh tubers are rich in Vitamin C, the amount going down during the time that they are in store. They also provide iron, calcium, thiamin, nicotinic acid, protein and fibre.

SITE, SOIL AND PLANTING

Aim for an open site on fertile, well-drained but moisture-retentive land that has been generously supplied with bulky organic material in a previous season. Avoid frost pockets where tender leaves may be killed on late spring nights. Rake in 3-4oz (75-100g) per sq yd (m) of general fertilizer before planting. This can be done in mid-March if weather permits, a fortnight earlier in warm regions, but later in northern gardens.

Buy certified seed tubers in mid-winter, ideally the size of a hen's egg, and stand them in a seed tray with the ends that have most eyes uppermost. Keep in a light, frost-free place to develop short sturdy shoots. Early potatoes should go in about 5in (13cm) deep and 10-12in (25-30cm) apart, with 20in (50cm) between rows.

It is easiest to plant potatoes with a trowel. Draw up some soil along each side of the row to make a slight ridge, and repeat to earth up the growing plants

Top: *Draw up some soil on each side of every row of young potato plants to earth them up to improve growth and tuber quality.*
Above: *Lift mature potatoes with a fork—taking care not to spear any of the tubers.*

once or twice during early growth to avoid green tubers and protect the foliage from frost.

On nights when frost is forecast, cover the plants with old newspapers. Water in dry spells throughout, but especially in the fortnight before harvest. Cloche cover helps give an early crop.

PESTS AND DISEASES

Blight does not usually affect first earlies, but avoid by cutting the tops off plants still growing in mid- to late summer. Avoid scab by adequate watering.

RHUBARB

Eaten as a fruit, but classified as a vegetable because we eat the leaf stalks, rhubarb is often relegated to a shady corner of the garden and, left to take care of itself, crops poorly. Given good treatment, the plants will provide abundant tender pink stems for pulling from late winter to early summer.

HISTORY

A native of Asia that was mentioned in a Chinese book on medicinal plants and herbs in 2700 BC, rhubarb was grown in the Middle Ages for medicinal use. Its popularity for pies and puddings dates back only to the 19th century.

FOOD VALUE

The stalks of rhubarb contain Vitamins A and C, mineral salts and dietary fibre.

SOWING AND PLANTING

Choose an open, sunny site, preferably on light rich soil. Dig deeply and manure generously before planting the crowns 3ft (90cm) apart with the buds just below soil level in mid-autumn to early spring. Rhubarb can be raised from seed, but this delays the first harvest and the quality of the crop is erratic.

AFTERCARE

Do not pull any stalks in the season after planting, and pull only a few the next spring. Water generously during dry spells, especially in the first year. Remove flower stems as soon as they appear. Top dress after the leaves have died down every autumn with a 2-3in (5-8cm) layer of rotted manure, and late every winter with 1-2oz (25-50g) per sq yd (m) of a quick-acting nitrogenous fertilizer.

A bed of rhubarb will grow for some years, but once the stalks become spindly and poo. the time has come to lift and divide the crowns, replanting some of the best portions.

FORCING RHUBARB

To obtain an early crop, lifted crowns can be taken indoors and 'forced', or grown artificially at an increased rate. The cut crowns are placed under covers and produce new stalks quickly, but have to be thrown away afterwards as they become useless in the process.

A better way is to force the crowns gently *in situ,* covering a clump or two in mid-winter with a thick pile of fallen leaves and an upturned dustbin, surrounded by more leaves or manure. This will give stalks for pulling some weeks before the uncovered crop, and does not spoil the crowns, but even so a clump should be forced only once in three years.

Upturned dustbin

Long-strawed manure and dead leaves

Pale leaves due to lack of light

Dead leaves

Above: *Tender early sticks of rhubarb are produced from plants gently forced in situ by covering early in the New Year with an upturned dustbin surrounded by straw, or fallen leaves, and manure. Cover a different plant next year.*

The different types of spinach seem alike when cooked, but the plants are not closely related and are usually listed in different parts of the seed catalogues. Grow annual spinach for early use, New Zealand spinach for summer, and spinach beet and chard for autumn and spring.

FOOD VALUE

A good source of Vitamins A and C, the leaves also provide calcium, iron, protein, potassium, folic acid and dietary fibre.

SITE, SOIL AND SOWING

The spinach tribe don't mind a bit of shade, and need a site that does not dry out in summer. Grow on land well supplied with bulky organic material and regularly limed. Rake 1oz (25g) of nitrogenous fertilizer into each sq yd (m) before spring sowings and give this as a top dressing to late sowings at the end of winter.

On dry soil, grow the New Zealand spinach. This is raised inside to go out, when frost risk is past, at 18in (45cm) each way, to trail over the ground for leaves to gather all summer. Sow annual spinach from late winter to late spring at three-week intervals, thinning seedlings to 6in (15cm) apart, perhaps with cloche cover for the first row, and give plenty of water or the plants may bolt. To overwinter, sow in late summer or early autumn and thin to 9in (22cm). Give cloche cover through the coldest months.

Spinach beet and Swiss chard are sown from mid-spring to mid-summer and thinned to 9in (22cm), to gather through summer, during spring, and in winter too if cloched.

PESTS AND DISEASES

Both seedlings and the over-wintered row may need netting as protection from birds in spring.

Above: *A rambling annual plant, New Zealand spinach is no relation of the other types. It will grow in hot dry conditions.*

Above: *Swiss chard has thick fleshy stalks that can be cooked separately, or with the leaf blades. Sow from mid-spring on.*

SWEET CORN

Sweet corn, a variety of maize, has become very popular in recent years. As the sugar in the kernels turns to starch after harvesting, flavour deteriorates, so shop-bought cobs can never equal those from the garden.

HISTORY

Maize was brought to Europe from America in the 16th century, but was regarded as stock feed until about 40 years ago.

FOOD VALUE

A source of protein, dietary fibre, mineral salts and trace elements, sweet corn also contains Vitamins A, C and some of the B group.

SOWING AND PLANTING

Choose a warm, sheltered site on deeply dug, fertile soil that has been supplied with rotted manure or compost in winter,

Above: *Corn cobs are ready to pick when the tassels have turned brown and grains are plump.*

and rake in 3-4oz (75-100g) of general fertilizer per sq yd (m). Sowing in the open gives too short a season, but seed can go under cloches or individual covers made from halved two-litre plastic soft drink bottles in late spring.

Grow corn in a block to assist pollination by wind at 12-18in (30-45cm) each way, the closer spacing for dwarf varieties. A better way is to raise plants inside, in individual 3in (8cm) pots to avoid root disturbance, to plant out under cloches in late spring.

In windy places corn may need staking, but usually drawing up some soil around the stems of young plants gives sufficient anchorage. Other crops can be grown in the half-shade between the corn as intercrops. Water well in dry weather after flowering, and liquid feed when cobs are swelling on poorer land.

Gather the cobs when their tassels have turned brown and a creamy fluid comes out of kernels pressed with a fingernail—a watery or very thick fluid indicates that cobs are too young or too old.

PESTS AND DISEASES

Bird and slug damage to young sweet corn is avoided by raising inside. Avoid fruit fly trouble by putting in plants which have already grown five or six leaves.

Above: *Sweet corn plants should be planted in a block rather than a row to ensure wind pollination of the flowers.*

TOMATOES

The tomato can be harvested from mid-summer to mid-autumn in the open garden if the plants are given an indoor start and protection in the first weeks outside. You don't have to buy plants, for seedlings are quite easy to raise on windowsills; and you can produce a crop in the smallest garden, as long as there is a sunny corner or wall.

HISTORY

Spaniards almost certainly brought tomato seed to Europe from South America, but it was 300 years later before the value of the fruit was realized, and plants began to be grown commercially. A supposed aphrodisiac property led to the old name of love apple.

FOOD VALUE

A good source of Vitamin C, the tomato also contains Vitamin A and, when raw, Vitamin E, plus folic acid, potassium, calcium and other mineral salts and trace elements, together with dietary fibre when both the skin and seeds are eaten.

SITE AND SOIL

Choose a sunny, sheltered site on good, well-drained, but moisture-retentive soil that was supplied with well rotted organic matter in the previous winter. A south-facing slope gives an ideal position for bush tomatoes and the staked plants do particularly well in front of a warm wall, or on the sunny side of a netting windbreak, or a sheltering row of tall beans. Rake 3-4oz (75-100g) per sq yd (m) of general fertilizer into the site before planting.

SOWING AND PLANTING

Sow seed in a pan of one part peat and one part sharp sand or perlite, in early spring on a warm windowsill indoors, and keep the compost moist until seedlings appear. Prick out as soon as the seed leaves have expanded, into individual 3in (8cm) pots of potting compost. Grow them on a cool windowsill until mid-spring, then move them to a cold frame for hardening off.

Plants cannot go out into the open until early summer except in warm areas, but can go out in late spring under cloches or when given some temporary

Below: *Tie growing tomato plants to their stakes every week, tying the stems below the flower trusses.*

Above: *Remove the small sideshoots from staked tomatoes regularly, pinching them off between thumb and forefinger.*

protection, perhaps with a large plastic bag for each seedling. Staked plants go in at 15in (37cm) apart and bush plants at 12-18in (30-45cm) depending on variety.

Bush plants are best planted through slits cut in black polythene sheet that will raise soil temperature, conserve moisture, keep down weeds and keep the fruits free of mud.

Remove cloches when flowering starts. Insert canes for staked tomatoes before planting to avoid root damage. Follow the planting directions given for tomatoes when using growing bags.

AFTERCARE

Water regularly in dry spells—an erratic water supply leads to split fruit. Remove sideshoots from staked plants while they are small and tie stems in every week. Remove the growing point in late summer, usually after 4-5 trusses of fruit have set, and also the lower leaves. Bush varieties are allowed to develop all shoots, but it is wise to remove some leaves in mid-summer to improve air circulation and assist ripening. Liquid-feed plants in growing bags and on poorer soil weekly from when the first fruit has set.

HARVEST

Gather fruits as they ripen until early autumn, when staked plants should be trimmed of all foliage, cut free and laid flat on polythene under cloches to help ripen the remaining green fruit. Cloches can go back over bush plants at this time. Fruit still green in mid-autumn can be picked and brought indoors to ripen on a cupboard shelf.

PESTS AND DISEASES

Blight is the curse of outdoor tomatoes, especially in a poor summer. Maintain a good air flow among plants and spray every two weeks from mid-summer with a copper fungicide as a preventative measure. Ripening fruit may need protecting from birds with netting.

Above: *Straw is laid around dwarf bush tomato plants to keep fruit clean. Planting through black polythene is another method.*

Above: *Staked outdoor tomato plants give fruit of equal quality to those grown in greenhouses. You may have to net against birds.*

TURNIPS AND SWEDES

Swedes are hardy roots for winter eating, which have grown in popularity in recent years. The first white turnips of summer make a good main vegetable, but otherwise the roots are needed more to bring out the flavour of other vegetables in stews and soups.

FOOD VALUE

Both crops provide Vitamin C and swedes also contain vitamins of the B group; turnip tops are a good source of Vitamin A as well. Mineral salts, trace elements and dietary fibre are also provided.

SITE, SOIL AND SOWING

Members of the cabbage family, swedes and turnips do best in alkaline conditions. They need ample moisture in the growing season and fertile soil. White turnips grow quickly, but remain in good condition for only a short time, and so only short rows should be grown. Sow seed thinly in early to mid-spring, thinning to 2in (5cm) apart, with 10in (25cm) between rows, to give roots for pulling in early to mid-summer.

Successional sowings can be made through the warm months, but it is more important to sow a hardy variety in late July to give roots to pull young in autumn and as needed through winter. Turnip seed can be sown in early autumn to give tops for eating in early spring, but these are too rank for most tastes.

Sow the slower-growing swedes in late spring/early summer, the earlier time in colder areas, with several seeds every 10in (25cm), and rows 15in (37cm) apart. Single to one per station for large roots to lift as needed from mid-autumn to early spring.

Swedes and turnips can both be stored for short periods, but are better used fresh from the garden. A few radish seeds can go in the swede drills as a catch crop to pull before the swedes need thinning.

PESTS AND DISEASES

Flea beetle is the most common pest and may make small holes in seed leaves, but damage is not usually severe. 'Marian' is a swede resistant to both club root and mildew.

Above: *'White Milan' turnip: an early variety with flattish roots.*

Above: *Single swedes to one per station at this size.*

Inspection of vegetable seed catalogues reveals a whole host of interesting ideas for salad crops. Some are not common in the shops, and a number of them are extremely simple to grow.

Broad-leaved endive: Sow in mid-summer and thin to 12in (30cm) apart, and blanch by covering mature plants, when the foliage is dry, with cloches darkened by black polythene, or individually with large upturned flower pots whose drainage holes have been covered to exclude light. The plants heart up much better than lettuce in autumn, but are prone to rot.

Corn salad: Sow in late summer and thin to 5in (13cm) apart each way. The forget-me-not-like rosettes of narrow shiny leaves are gathered individually in winter and spring. Also called lamb's lettuce, it should be given cloche cover to encourage new leaves to grow in the colder months. Its main use is in early spring salads.

Land cress: Sow this perennial, also called American cress, on fertile, moisture-retentive soil in spring or summer to give rosettes of rich-green leaves, with a flavour like watercress. These may be gathered individually for salads over many months. Cover in winter to encourage growth through the cold months.

Moss-curled endive: Sow in early to mid-summer and thin to 10in (25cm) for small heads of fringed leaves. These must be blanched before they are sweet enough to eat. Cover only a few plants at a time, as blanched endive soon deteriorates. It is less hardy than the broad-leaved type, and will not go on so long into autumn. Both are prone to bolting if sown before mid-summer.

Mung bean shoots: These are the easiest and quickest of several seeds that can be sprouted in large jam jars or instant coffee jars laid on their sides on a shelf or windowsill indoors. They must be kept moist and rinsed in clean water twice a day. The nutritious shoots are ready to eat in four to five days. Alfalfa, fenugreek and

Below: *Moss-curled endive makes a pleasant change from lettuce, but it must be blanched before eating.*

Top: *The outer leaves of Red Verona chicory conceal dense pink-coloured chicons.*

Above: *Parsley is a firm favourite in the kitchen, both as a salad vegetable and as a garnish.*

alphatoco beans can also be sprouted in this way.

Mustard and cress: Sow on shallow trays of peat indoors, or in growing bags or trays in the greenhouse. Keep dark until the seedlings are about 1½in (4cm) high. Uncover for a few days to allow the leaves to expand and turn green before cutting. Mustard can be equally well grown in a greenhouse border, or in the open garden, if covered with an upturned seed tray or box until the seedlings are well up.

Treat cress in the same way as mustard, but allow four more days between sowing and harvest. Alternatively, sow in broad shallow drills in the open, under cloches or in the greenhouse border, to grow on until ferny true leaves have developed. They make a tasty and unusual leaf salad.

Parsley: Sow this biennial on good moisture-retentive soil from early spring to mid-summer, or start it inside to transplant into the open at 5in (13cm) apart. Give cloche cover through the winter for a continuous supply of young leaves for salad. Best grown in a row or block near a path to allow fresh foliage to be gathered for the kitchen in all weathers.

Radishes: Sow seed thinly in short broad drills, or sprinkled in with the seed of slower

maturing vegetables, every three weeks from early spring to late summer (from late winter under cloches). Fertile soil and regular watering are important to ensure quick growth and mild tender roots. Given this radishes will be ready to pull in four weeks from sowing in the warmer summer months.

Red Verona chicory: Grown in the same way as Sugar Loaf, this less usual Italian chicory makes shorter, rounder heads that will stand more frost—but they also benefit from cloche cover to extend the season. The green leaves turn to red with the onset of cold weather, and the peeled chicons are an attractive pink.

Salad onions: Sow in short broad drills every three to four weeks from late winter to late summer (and in early autumn using a winter hardy strain). This will give a succession of slim onions to pull green from early spring until well into autumn. The first sowing of the year will develop far more quickly if given cloche cover.

Sugar Loaf chicory: Sow in early to mid-summer and thin to 10in (25cm) apart to make self-folding heads that are ready from mid-autumn to mid-winter, going on longer into winter if given cloche cover. When the outer leaves are stripped away there are large solid chicons to eat straight from the garden.

Winter radishes: Sow these larger, hotter varieties of radish in mid-summer and thin to 2in (5cm) apart to pull round, cylin-drical or long roots with black, red or white skins and white flesh from mid-autumn to early spring. Lift and store the roots, or leave them in the ground and cover with 2in (5cm) of peat to protect them from frost and lift as needed.

Left: *Radishes (top), salad onions (centre) and winter radishes (bottom) are all excellent crops for odd corners of the garden.*

73

RECOMMENDED VARIETIES

This is a selection from the many competing varieties on the market. Criteria include easy, trouble-free growing, good yields, convenient timing or length of season, and storage qualities.

Globe Artichoke: 'Green Globe'.
Jerusalem Artichoke: Silver-skinned; 'Fuseau'.
Asparagus: Modern hybrids 'Lorella' and 'Lucullus'.
Broad beans: 'Aquadulce' for mid-autumn sowing; 'Jubilee Hysor', 'Relon' and 'Witkiem Major' for late winter or early spring sowing. 'The Sutton' is a dwarf to sow under cloches at either time.
French beans: 'Pros Gitana' and 'Delinel' are dwarf and 'Largo' is a climber. 'Chevrier Vert' can be grown for green beans, or pods can be ripened to dry as haricot beans for winter.
Runner beans: 'Hammond's Dwarf Scarlet' and 'Gulliver' are dwarf; the early 'Kelvedon Marvel' can be pinched out as a dwarf or grown as a climber; 'Achievement', 'Prizewinner', 'Red Knight', and 'Streamline' are climbers.

Beetroot: 'Avonearly' and 'Boltardy' are bolt-resistant varieties for early sowing; the cylindrical 'Forono', and 'Cylindra', the long 'Cheltenham Green Top', and round 'Detroit New Globe' will store well; use 'Detroit Little Ball' for mid-summer sowing.
Broccoli: Both purple and white sprouting come in early and late strains; 'Nine Star' can be perennial; 'Express Corona', 'Green Comet' and 'Corvet' are calabrese, as is the lighter green 'Romanesco', to harvest later in autumn.
Brussels sprouts: The dwarf 'Peer Gynt' for harvesting from early autumn to early spring; 'Citadel' and 'Widgeon' F1 hybrids for mid-season and 'Achilles' and 'Rampart' for use from early winter.
Cabbage: For summer the pointed 'Hispi' and ball-headed 'Marner Allfrüh', followed by 'Minicole' or 'Stonehead' that both

Above: *'Boltardy' (top) is a bolt-resistant variety of beetroot suitable for sowing early in the season. 'Sugar Snap' (centre) is a tall mange-tout or sugar pea. 'Model White' (bottom) is a popular round white turnip variety.*

stand well; for autumn and winter the red 'Langedijker Early'—'Norma', winter white 'Jupiter', savoy 'Ice Queen' and late 'Winter King', smoother-leaved 'Celtic' and 'January King' type 'Aquarius'; for spring the pointed 'Hispi', or 'Pixie', or round 'Spring Hero'. Chinese cabbage: 'Nagaoka 50 Days' or 'Tip Top'.

Carrots: For the protected crop 'Amsterdam Forcing', for early outdoor sowing 'Nantes Express', for the maincrop 'Berlicum—Berjo', or 'Autumn King Vita Longa'. On shallow soils grow 'Kundulus' and 'Chantenay Red Cored'.

Cauliflower: For early summer 'Mechelse—Delta', followed by 'Dominant', mini cauliflower; for late summer 'Dok Elgon'; for autumn 'Mill Reef', 'Canberra'; for spring 'Angers No 2—Westmarsh Early', 'Walcheren Winter' series 'Markanta' and 'Birchington', and 'English Winter—Late Queen'.

Celery: 'Celebrity', or 'Lathom Self-blanching'; 'Giant White', 'Giant Pink' or 'Giant Red' trenched celery—the red is the hardiest; 'Marble Ball' and 'Tellus' celeriac.

Cucumbers: F1 hybrids 'Burpless Tasty Green', 'Sweet Success' (all female and good for frames) and 'Tokyo Slicer'.

Kale: 'Dwarf Curly' and 'Fribor', 'Pentland Brig'.

Leeks: 'Autumn Giant—Herwina' and 'Giant Winter—Cataline'.

Lettuce: See successional lettuce sowing chart (page 54).

Marrows etc: 'Chefini', 'Early Gem' and 'Zucchini' for courgettes or marrows. 'Golden Delicious' is a trailer with golden top-shaped fruits to store. "Atlantic Giant" produces huge pumpkins.

Onions: Round 'Sturon' and flat 'Stuttgarter Giant' sets for spring planting, Suttons 'Autumn' and Unwins 'First Early' for autumn planting. The flagon-shaped 'Hative de Niort' and 'Long-Keeping Yellow' shallots. 'Paris Silverskin' and 'The Queen' pickling onions. 'Hygro' and 'Rijnsburger—Balstora' seed to sow in spring for maincrop bulbs to store; 'Solidity' to sow in late summer, 'Ailsa Craig' to sow in mid-winter, for planting out in spring. 'Express Yellow O-X' is for late summer sowing.

Parsnips: 'Avonresister' and 'White Gem' are dumpy and resistant to canker.

Peas: 'Feltham First' and 'Meteor' are hardy round-seeded peas; 'Hurst Beagle', 'Kelvedon Wonder', and 'Little Marvel' first early dwarf are all wrinkled-seeded; 'Hurst Green Shaft' and 'Onward' are second earlies of medium height; 'Alderman' and 'Senator' are tall maincrop peas; 'Edula' is a medium height plant and 'Sugar Snap' is a tall sugar pea. 'Poppet' is a self-supporting dwarf to grow in deep beds.

Potatoes: 'Maris Bard' is very early. 'Dunluce' and 'Ulster Sceptre' are also useful early varieties.

Rhubarb: 'Timperley Early' is a good forcing variety.

Spinach: Sow 'Norvak' in spring or late summer, or 'Symphony' in spring.

Sweet corn: 'Aztec', 'Earlibelle', and 'Kelvedon Sweetheart' F1 Hybrids.

Tomatoes: 'Red Alert' for compact early bushes and 'Alfresco' also dwarf; 'Alicante' for staked tomatoes; 'Gardener's Delight' for very sweet small fruit and 'Marmande' for extra large fruit for slicing and cooking.

Turnips and swedes: 'Early Snowball', 'White Milan' and 'Model White' are popular early varieties for spring sowing, and 'Green Top Stone' for mid-summer. 'Marian' is the best swede.

Other salads: 'Batavian Broadleaved' and 'Moss Curled' endive; 'Extra Double Curled Cress'; 'White Lisbon' and 'Winter Bunching' salad onions; 'Cherrybelle' and 'French Breakfast' radish; 'Black Spanish', 'China Rose' and 'Mino Early' winter radish; 'Sugar Loaf', 'Crystal Head' and Red Verona chicory; 'Moss Curled' parsley.

INDEX

PICTURE CREDITS

Artists
Copyright of the artwork illustrations on the pages following the artists' names is the property of Salamander Books Ltd.
Stuart Lafford (Linden Artists): 36, 39, 40, 46, 60
Janos Marffy: 50 (both)
Dee McLean (Linden Artists): 11, 12, 16-17, 21, 30, 34, 38, 47, 65

Photographers
The publishers wish to thank the following photographers who have supplied photographs for this book. The photographs have been credited by page number, and position on the page where appropriate: B (Bottom), T (Top), BL (Bottom Left) etc.
Eric Crichton: Endpapers, 4-5, 6, 8, 14, 15, 18, 19, 20, 22, 24, 28, 29 (T), 31, 32, 33, 35, 37, 41, 42, 43, 44, 45, 46, 48, 49, 51, 52, 53, 54, 57 (L), 58, 59, 60, 61, 62, 63, 64, 66, 67, 68, 69, 71, 73 (T,C), 74 (T,C), Cover
Neil Holmes: 29 (B), 56, 57 (R), 70, 72, 73 (B), 74 (B)
Michael Warren: 38